Sketching Stories, Stretching Minds

Sketching Stories, Stretching Minds

Responding Visually to Literature

Phyllis Whitin

HEINEMANN
Portsmouth, NH

HEINEMANN
A division of Reed Elsevier Inc.
361 Hanover Street
Portsmouth, NH 03801-3912
Offices and agents throughout the world

The author and publisher are grateful to the following for permission to reprint previously published material:
The dedication is an allusion to the poem "He Wishes for the Cloths of Heaven," from *The Complete Poems of W.B. Yeats*, 1956. New York: The Macmillan Publishing Company, Inc.
Excerpts from Chapter 1 originally appeared as "Opening Potential: Visual Response to Literature." *Language Arts*, February, 1994. Copyright 1994 by National Council of Teachers of English. Reprinted with permission.
Portions of Chapters 4 and 6 are a revision of "Visual Response to Literature: Exploring the Potential of Meaning-Making." *Research in the Teaching of English*, (February, 1996). Copyright 1996 by National Council of Teachers of English. Reprinted with permission.

Library of Congress Cataloging-in-Publication Data
Whitin, Phyllis.
Sketching stories, stretching minds / Phyllis Whitin.
p.   cm.
Includes bibliographical references (p.   ).
ISBN 0-435-08870-X
1. Literature—Study and teaching (Elementary)   2. Drawing—Study and teaching (Elementary).   3. Reader—response criticism.   4. English language—Composition and exercises—Study and teaching (Elementary)
I. Title.
LB1576.W486283   1996
372'.64'044—dc20   95-40134
                                                                    CIP

Editor: Scott Mahler
Consulting editor: Maureen Barbieri
Production: J. B. Tranchemontagne
Manufacturing: Louise Richardson
Cover design: Michael Leary

Printed in the United States of America on acid-free paper

Docutech RRD 2005

To my husband, David
who gives me the heavens' embroidered cloths

Contents

Foreword

Years ago when my daughter Alison was one of the informants in our studies of what young children know about reading and writing prior to going to school (Harste, Woodward, and Burke 1984), she stopped by my college classroom to catch a ride home. I loved the comment she made as she was helping me clean up, "I hope someday I have a college class where the last thing the professor says is, 'Be sure to put your crayons away!'"

We had a good laugh, and then reflected on how sad it was that you don't find easels in every single classroom in school. Most people see crayons as something for young children, but not necessary tools for middle school, high school, college students or adults. "They simply don't believe what I believe, and what you taught me," I said. It was one of those unforgettable moments when a whole new world opened up to me.

I remember a phone conversation six-year-old Alison had with her friend Jennifer. They were going to "play ballerina" after church. Alison would get her leotard, slippers, and hair ribbons from her dresser, and Jennifer would bring her leotard, slippers, and hair ribbons with her in a bag from church. When Alison got off the phone, she went to her room and recorded her conversations. She used art, math, and language to do so.

Initially, I was struck by the simple elegance of Alison's product. To take a complex literacy event and reduce it so elegantly seemed like the work of a powerful authoring mind. And the more I thought about it, the more impressed I became. Literacy is much more than reading and writing. Broadly defined, it's the process by which we mediate the world for the purpose of learning. To mediate the world means to create sign systems—mathematics, art, music, dance, language—that stand between the world as it is and the world as we perceive it. These sign systems act as lenses that permit us better to understand ourselves and our world.

Taking what we know in one sign system and recasting it in terms of another is both natural and basic to literacy. What Alison did by taking her phone conversation and representing it visually is a natural instance of sketch-to-stretch, as well as an instance of a more generalizable process called transmediation. Sketch-to-stretch is an instructional strategy—some might even call it an instructional intervention—but it is important to know that, at base, all it does is invite language users to do and to bring to conscious awareness what the mind does naturally. I see metaphor as the basic process of the mind. Metaphor, for me, is the base of all cognition and hence learning, curriculum, and education. It is also the key process under-lying sketch-to-stretch (Siegel 1995), and why Phyllis Whitin is absolutely right in making it the central focus of her curriculum.

Literacy, like metaphor, always involves a leap of faith. It is not good enough just to make meaning of text. Literacy demands more. One has to see the meaning that was made metaphorically and ask what new things are explained about the world and how it works. In a community of learners this process is generative, exciting, and, as Phyllis Whitin demonstrates, downright invigorating for students, teachers, and how we think about the process of schooling.

Sketching Stories, Stretching Minds is a marvelous book. Phyllis Whitin shows us what happens when we dare envision curriculum as a metaphor for the lives we want to live and the people we want to be. She explores how sign systems might be used to disrupt the current "texts" that students hold for books and literacy. In the process she disrupts our "texts" and demonstrates that what we invite students to do in classrooms makes a real difference in terms of creating more thoughtful and more literate worlds.

I wanted to start here. I think the function of a good Foreword is to put things into perspective. What Alison did for me, Phyllis Whitin takes further and does for readers. This is teacher research at its best. The participants speak my kind of English:

"Visuals help me see things in a new way." *Abby, Grade 7*

"Sometimes the craziest idea can get you the farthest." *David, Grade 7*

"So I'm saying that when you're in an authors' circle for visuals, you get ideas, and you revise it [your visual] just like a writer." *Seth, Grade 7*

"I have found that teacher research does not mean 'doing' some-thing to kids. Instead, teacher research is looking closely, listening attentively, and learning collaboratively with my students." *Phyllis Whitin, Grade 7 Teacher*

Here are what I see as the text's highlights:

It's Practical. Sketch-to-stretch is a simple instructional strategy that you can use come Monday morning. Better yet, it is one of those strategies that can be played with and that can grow over time, in the end significantly enhancing and reforming the English Language Arts curriculum as we know it.

It's Thoughtful. With example after example of student learning, the book demonstrates all of the educational potentials that open up when other sign systems are made available in curriculum. Art, I think, is sometimes the most poorly taught subject in schools. Too often it is used for presentational purposes after all of the thinking is done. In *Sketching Stories, Stretching Minds*, Phyllis Whitin and her students demonstrate how to use art and other sign systems to support all of the underlying processes in learning, including conversation, observation, and reflection.

It's Transformative. The students in Phyllis Whitin's seventh-grade English classes read hundreds of books. There were two catches, however. They read thoughtfully and they read with a crayon in their hand. In some ways *Sketching Stories, Stretching Minds* can be read as an argument for why crayons, easels, and yes, even great pieces of art, graphs, and good quality musical instruments (I'm extending the argument!) should be in every seventh grade classroom. If middle school teachers don't go out and buy an easel or at least have their students buy a box of simple markers after they read this book, I'll have to revise my sketch of what effect I envision this book will have!

It Hits the Right Audience. I particularly like *Sketching Stories, Stretching Minds* because of who it is written for. Too many books in the past have been written for elementary teachers with the assumption that middle school teachers should read them and "adapt." Phyllis Whitin turns the table on us. Here is a book for middle school teachers that early childhood, elementary, secondary, and college teachers should read! "Just adapt! There is nothing to it!"

It's Teaching at Its Best. Phyllis Whitin positions herself as a teacher researcher with the students acting as co-investigators. The thoughtful discussions as well as the careful probing to understand are lessons in the art and science of teaching and inquiry. There is no "Cha-Cha-Cha Curriculum" here (Graves 1983), but rather the evolution of education through thoughtful and focused inquiry.

It's Education as It Should Be. The more I am involved in inquiry with children, the more I am convinced that it is not good enough just to have children experience inquiry. They need to have opportunities and support to bring what they know to conscious awareness. Once what they know is made conscious, it can be acted upon and researched. In sketch-to-stretch the visuals become a reflective tool for understanding knowing in this deeper way. Just as literacy involves flexibility in the use of sign systems, so reflection and articulation (visual as well as oral) are integral parts of the learning process. Nothing I have read so vividly demonstrates these points as does *Sketching Stories, Stretching Minds*. The stories it contains are a virtual handbook on learning. The book itself is a vivid demonstration of why teachers need to write. Phyllis Whitin's book stands as a testimonial to why we are a poorer profession when curriculums remain unwritten.

I really like this book. It's both timely and long overdue. Unlike language in which ideas must be developed linearly, art provides a view of the whole as well as how all the parts fit together. I'll open discussion of *Sketching Stories, Stretching Minds* by using one of the many clever variants that Phyllis Whitin and the students in her classroom explored using sketch-to-stretch. In this instance, I'll use Alison's old sketch as a personal but symbolic sketch of what this book meant to me as well as share with you my interpretation:

Overall, the book stands as an invitation to try a new "dance." The plus symbolizes that teachers and students can do this collaboratively. The inclusion of each participant's set of initials means that we can personalize our use of this strategy in ways that best fit us and the perspectives we have. The net result: sheer curricular eloquence.

Your turn. Read. Sketch. Discuss. The possibilities are endless.

Jerome C. Harste
Indiana University

References

GRAVES, D. 1983. *Writing: Teachers and Children at Work*. Portsmouth, NH: Heinemann.

HARSTE, J. C., WOODWARD, V. A., AND BURKE, C. L. 1984. *Language Stories and Literacy Lessons*. Portsmouth, NH: Heinemann.

SIEGEL, M. 1995. "More than Words: The Generative Power of Transmediation in Learning," *Canadian Journal of Education* 95:1, 24–38.

Acknowledgments

I feel an enormous sense of gratitude for the countless people who have contributed to this work through conversations, guidance, and shared experiences. Heidi Mills's perceptive eye enabled me to see the significance of classroom events as I collected and analyzed data. She helped me to connect theory and practice in a way that deepened my understanding of the processes of learning. Carolyn Burke and Marjorie Siegel also gave me invaluable advice by helping me to frame my study. It was their suggestions that encouraged me to invite students to join me in my research. These seventh graders taught me more than they will ever realize, and I appreciate each of them as well.

I am grateful to Maureen Barbieri, my consulting editor at Heinemann, who guided me as only the best writing teacher can, by encouraging me to find my own voice to tell my story. Her belief in teacher research and in the middle school learner spurred me on. I also wish to thank Joanne Tranchemontagne for her expertise in directing the production of this book. I appreciate her time in listening to my many suggestions. Finally, this book would not have been written without the years of learning together with my husband, David. I appreciate his helping me to form my thoughts through conversations, responding to every draft, and believing in my potential.

Introduction

Visuals help me see things in a new way.
ABBY, GRADE 7

My interest in sketching, like all good teaching adventures, was inspired by students. I was familiar with the sketch-to-stretch strategy of Harste, Short and Burke (1988), but students made its potential come alive. The strategy is described as sketching what the story means to a reader. I was intrigued with the idea that colors, shapes and symbols might convey the feelings, themes, and ideas in reading even though I have no artistic training myself. For several years I assigned a poetry project in which students created a sketch to accompany a poem of their choice. The sketches served as a personal interpretation of the theme of the poem.

One year, however, Chris taught me a new lesson about sketching. The class had read *Summer of the Monkeys*, and all the students made posters as a culminating project. "I can't draw," Chris told me as he unrolled his poster, "so I did something different for my project." I looked as Chris explained his work. His sketch was a simple outline of a square with a triangle on top, rather like a stylized house shape. In each corner and in the center of the "house," Chris had painted a dark blue square with an interior yellow square. Dotted green lines connected all five yellow/blue squares. Chris told me that the yellow squares symbolized the main characters of the novel. The square in the center stood for Daisy, the sister of the narrator, because "She linked everyone together." Chris read the commentary for his poster aloud: "The black stands for danger and sadness. Yet the yellow and green stand for the bonded relationship which stands through the darkness and shines bright through the story."

Of all the projects I saw that day, Chris's is the one that has stayed with me. It impressed me for two reasons. First, the sketch was condensed; it conveyed several major ideas about the book in a small space: Chris had considered theme, character relationships, mood, conflict, and conflict resolution. Secondly, his sketch expressed Chris's feelings and the feelings of the characters in the book. When Chris shared his poster with his classmates, his sketch served as an invitation for deep discussion. I began to wonder how sketching could be used as a tool for understanding reading in our day-to-day experiences with literature. We were already using reader's response journals to record our thinking as we read. Why not use a symbolic system to interpret literature?

Collaboration with adults in a graduate class I was teaching opened my eyes to another important part of this strategy. I confessed to the members of this class that I felt something was missing from my work with sketching. I described how I normally used the sketching strategy as a culminating project that was completed at home. Theresa, one of the teachers in the class, recognized that this approach was inconsistent with Writers' Workshop or the authoring cycle. She wondered aloud, "Why not provide time to share drafts of sketches in authors' circles? We always share our writing in process." Theresa's comment paved the way for me to examine sketching as a parallel process to writing. We create in similar ways despite the medium we employ. When I combined Chris's ideas with Theresa's, I began to capitalize upon sketching in new and exciting ways. I had learned an important lesson about teacher research: Share my thinking and my questions with both adults and young people.

This book, then, is two-pronged in its intent. First, I am sharing a strategy that I believe holds rich potential for understanding literature. There is always a danger in written response to literature; it is easy to slip into retelling or summarizing events of a story. By sketching, one is forced to interpret the literature, especially when we define sketching as using symbols, color, and line to show the ideas or feelings in a story. Often sketches are like Chris's poster, a geometric arrangement of colors and lines rather than a realistic drawing. Since there is no single definition for a color or a shape, members of a group generate new interpretations as they discuss a sketch.

Secondly, I am sharing my thinking as a teacher in this book. I believe in the power of teacher research. The heart of educational renewal lies in the classroom. I have read a lot of theory and usually find it to be helpful and logical, but it only becomes real when I see these concepts emerge from my work with children. I have grown as a teacher by looking closely at classroom events and by inviting students to share their thinking with me. The students became my partners in learning; I have asked them to react to my wonderings and tentative hypotheses. I have found that teacher research does not mean "doing" something *to* kids. Instead, teacher research is looking closely, listening attentively, and learning collaboratively with my students. Through teacher research we not only see established theory come alive, but we also generate new theory.

This book is organized to pursue these two dimensions. In the first chapter I introduce the sketching strategy through one literary study that took place in the beginning of an academic year—most of the stories in the book follow this same group of children. As I began to look closely at the sketching strategy in the day-to-day classroom life, I found it helpful to refer to the authoring cycle model (Harste, et. al. 1988). This model helped me to see the relationship between sketching and writing that Theresa had suggested. Chapter 2 explores this relationship. Certain features of authoring and of classroom life in general seemed to be crucial to the spirit of inquiry that I was trying to foster in the classroom. Chapter 3 describes strategies to develop these features. In Chapter 4 I look closely at the way in which a class developed an idea for sketching through discussion and experimentation. Chapter 5 tells the story of one student, Doug, who taught me important lessons about the role of risk-taking in learning. Chapter 6 describes a new role of sketching that I discovered through collaboration with my colleagues and with students. Sketching can be a powerful tool for reflection, both for individuals as we look at ourselves as learners, and as a collaborative community as we examine the nature of learning itself.

There are several aspects that I do *not* address in depth in the book, and it is likely that readers will wonder about them. First, is sketching a requirement? What about students who do not like the sketching strategy? I only require individual sketches once in a given academic year, as I describe in the first chapter. After we use the strategy together once, sketching becomes one choice for responding in their journals. Some students are initially afraid that they will be judged for their artistic ability: they frequently take the risk to sketch later in the year after they see their classmates sketch abstract ideas through graphs and abstract designs. Others choose not to sketch in their journals at any time. However, these students collaborate with small groups for special sketching projects, and they contribute ideas to class discussions of other people's sketches. I have asked several of these students why they chose not to sketch in their journals, and their answers have helped me understand the sketching strategy in new ways. For example, one boy explained to me that he appreciated the way that sketches generated lots of ideas in a group discussion about a story, but he was reluctant to create sketches on his own: "If you sketch, people have questions for other meanings, and you have to keep explaining it." He would rather write a response, which he felt generated fewer questions and alternative interpretations, than create a sketch.

Readers will also wonder about grading. How can a teacher grade a sketch? Students write brief commentaries about their sketches so that I can see their thinking in more than one way, and I treat the sketches as I do any other reader's response. I expect students to respond thoughtfully and personally in their journals. Their ideas should extend the ideas in their reading, and they should demonstrate a clear connection to the content of the story. I grade entries on these criteria, using a scale of 0–5 points. A five-point entry shows extensive thought, while a zero stands for missing work. The other points show values between these two extremes. At the end of the grading period I add the scores together to convert to a letter journal grade. I use a rubric that elaborates upon these same features to evaluate more elaborate sketches for culminating novel projects, and I ask students to self-evaluate as part of their grade.

Another question involves the issue of time. I was fortunate to have two periods allotted for language arts in my seventh-grade class, and that luxury allowed for more discussion time than in single-period schedules. However, like all teachers, I constantly wrestled with the issue of using time wisely. I did not "add on" sketching to our already busy schedule. Sketching was one of the many forms of reader response, and we were already using literature circles to discuss journal entries. The one addition to our previous schedule was sharing sessions about the strategy itself. In Chapter 4 readers will see that at first I was afraid to talk about our process of learning during class time. As I listened closely to the students' comments, I realized that these class discussions gave students the opportunity to understand themselves better as learners. They became empowered, independent learners as they took charge of the strategy in personal ways. Giving time to reflect about learning as a group is one of the most important lessons I have learned through this teaching adventure.

What about these kids? Are they really typical? In some ways they are, and in some ways, they are not. When I investigated the sketching strategy in depth, I taught both of the language arts classes. One period was devoted to Writers' Workshop, and those classes were heterogeneously grouped. The other class centered on literature study, and those groups were homogeneously grouped. I was assigned to teach literature to those students who were labeled as academically gifted, and it is their work that is found in this book. However, I have used the sketching strategy with students who were labeled average, below average, or as special learners. (I feel uncomfortable with these labels, but these were the terms that were used to form the composition of my classes.) This strategy has been equally helpful with all students. I currently teach a heterogeneous fourth grade class, and find sketching exciting in this setting as well.

Finally, I do not address the down side of teaching. Yes, I have my bad days and, of course, frustrations in day-to-day classroom life.

I get discouraged. However, when I think about all of my experiences with sketching as a response to reading, I don't have any disappointing or frustrating stories. Reflecting upon this idea, I realized that we, as teachers, burn out, when our teaching becomes predictable, when the teacher's manual tells us what answers to expect. Sketching is full of surprises and unanticipated outcomes. There never is a right or a wrong sketch; each challenges us to think in new ways. Abby explained this idea when she said, "Visuals help me see things in a new way." Her comment applies to me as a teacher, as well as to her as a student. Through sketching she sees books in new ways, and so do I. If we continue to think in new ways, we will always be growing, and we will always stay refreshed.

ONE

Summer of the Monkeys

When you make a visual, first you think long and hard about different connections. Then you 'draw' your idea on paper and put meaning into it. Your friends and teachers help you.

CARA, *Grade 7*

Seventh graders who enter my class each August have usually responded to literature by answering teacher- or text-generated questions, most of which have implied one correct answer. In order to encourage students to entertain the idea of personal interpretation of literature, I lead the group through a shared experience using the strategy of sketch-to-stretch within the first few days of school. The experience is based upon a powerful short story such as "All Summer in a Day" by Ray Bradbury, which describes a community living on Venus, where it rains constantly except for one hour every seven years. Margot, the main character, is the only child in her class who remembers the sun, since she lived on Earth until she was four. In the story the children viciously lock Margot in the closet, and she misses the one hour of sunshine. It is a story that evokes strong feelings and images, qualities that have rich potential for intense and varied responses. Our lesson on Bradbury's story goes something like this:

1

First, we think hard about a long period of rain. We imagine the sky, we listen for the constant pounding of rain, and we sense the feeling of being restricted from outdoor activity. Of course, we acknowledge that rain can be comforting, relaxing, and soothing, but we imagine rain for extended periods of time. Each of us sketches, lists or writes about the images and feelings that come to mind. Next I explain that after I read the story aloud, no one will talk. We will quietly return to our reader's response journals and capture our immediate impressions on paper. Next, I read the story while students rest their heads on their desks or lie on the floor. I pause after the last sentence, and then whisper for everyone to respond in the journals. After we have responded and shared our ideas orally, I explain the strategy of sketch-to-stretch as a process of reacting to theme, characters and their relationships, conflict, and feelings through sketching symbols, colors, shapes, lines, and textures. I emphasize that we do not need to be artists to sketch our feelings and ideas. We return to "All Summer in a Day," and I ask, "What is an important idea in this story?" A typical answer is the feeling of despair. In one class the conversation continued in this way.

"Despair. Okay, how could we convey the feeling of despair in a shape? Theresa?"

"Have a flower all drooped over," Theresa suggests.

"Is there a color to suggest despair?" I ask.

"Gray," replies Jacob.

"Jacob has suggested gray. Was anyone thinking of any other color besides gray that might symbolize despair?"

We continue the discussion by thinking of other colors, shapes, and symbols that could be used to signify despair as well as other feelings or themes in the story. I want to demonstrate that there are many alternatives that can be used to signify each idea. What is important is that the author of the idea has a reason in mind for the choice of symbol. For the initial experience, I ask that students create a sketch-to-stretch in their reader's response journals for homework. I want the students to discover the power of extending meaning through conversations about the sketches during the next day's class.

As class begins the following day, the students form small groups and share their sketches. Sometimes I have asked the authors of the sketches to share by using the "Save the Last Word for Me" strategy (Harste, et. al., 1988). In this strategy, the author simply places the visual in view of the rest of the group. Members of the group study the sketch and tell the author what they notice, such as, "When you used the broken line between the gray and the yellow, I thought how Margot was separated from the sun." After each person has contributed an idea, the author explains her own reasoning. After all members have shared ideas in each group, we assemble as a class once more. I invite group members to nominate their peers to share their sketches with the entire class. Individuals have the right to decline the nomination, but almost everyone accepts with pleasure. Those who nominated a friend explain what they appreciated about their peer's sketch. In this way we start to build community by encouraging class members to be comfortable in acknowledging what they learned from each other. I often show my sketch and explain how past students have inspired me.

After a number of students have had the opportunity to share their ideas, we talk about questions like, "In what ways have these sketches enabled you to see something in the story that you had not seen when you first heard the story aloud yesterday?" I want students to see that through sharing ideas, our personal views are broadened and deepened. For example, one student, Michelle, used a block of blue and gray to stand for the rain, which surrounded a smaller block of yellow. The yellow stood for the little bit of brightness that Margot, the main character, felt when she thought about the sun. Beneath the two blocks, Michelle colored a band of gray that symbolized the character's being sad and lonely since the other kids were jealous of her. When she showed the class her sketch, she explained, "The children were envious and angry at Margot." Will then spoke up to say, "I never thought of the other kids' jealousy before."

Theresa exclaimed as she flipped through her book to find a reference, "Of course they were jealous. They hadn't ever seen the sun, and Margot had."

In every class comments such as Will's and Theresa's serve as springboards for class reflection. We spend a few minutes as a class thinking back on the process of creating and sharing. We talk about generating new meanings through collaboration. Without Michelle's visual, Will might not have thought about the children's jealousy toward Margot. Theresa, on the other hand, had probably considered the feeling of jealousy, but the conversation encouraged her to revisit the text to find a specific reference to build upon Michelle's idea. This reflective conversation helps class members learn that collaboration leads to the creation of new ideas and understanding. I want to establish this feeling of interdependence early in the year. Since there are always many types of sketches, we also establish the idea that there are multiple interpretations to any piece of literature and that each can be justified in various ways.

After this class exploration, I invite students to respond to literature by sketching in their journals. Sometimes they choose to respond individually in class or at home. Other times they sketch while sitting with the members of their literature circles, thereby benefiting from collaboration during the process of composing. Students can also sketch collaboratively or individually as a culminating response to a literary study. During our first novel study of the year students explore each of these choices. A look at one particular group's novel study can demonstrate how these ideas look in action.

An Overview of a Literary Study

Seventh-grade students are required to read various works of literature through the course of the year. The school also has multiple copies of novels to offer as choices for literary studies. Because I believe that student choice is important, I begin the year with a novel study based upon several of the optional novels. One of these books is *Summer of the Monkeys* (Rawls 1976).

With this particular group, I offered Rawls's book and *All Together Now* (Bridgers 1979) as choices. On the day before our actual literary study began, copies of each of the novels were on display. We discussed Wilson Rawls's work: He wrote *Summer of the Monkeys* in 1976 as well as *Where the Red Fern Grows* in 1961. *Summer of the Monkeys* is set in the Ozark Mountains in the early twentieth century. The main problem of the story is that Jay Berry, a fourteen-year-old boy, tries to capture some escaped circus monkeys in order to get a cash reward.

We talked about both books. Students then wrote down their choice of novels. That night I reviewed the requests and set up groups of students who would work together, four to a group, though some groups were smaller because of choices in the class. When the students arrived the next day, I passed out their books. I then asked that by the end of the period the groups collaborate and develop a time frame outlining when they planned to read certain sections and when they planned to discuss their journals. After hearing the instructions, the groups selected places to sit. Some were at tables, some pushed together desks, and some took carpet squares to scatter on the floor. I had written *Reader's Response* on the board for homework. The students could reflect about their reading in their reader's response journals in whatever way they felt would best help their enjoyment and understanding of the book. They might copy a favorite passage and describe why they liked it; they might make predictions from their initial readings or write or sketch about how they felt as a reader.

Over the next few days I circulated around the room, responding in writing to journal entries, listening to conversations, and occasionally asking a question to extend the dialogue among the members of a group. Listening to conversations, I found points or ideas that study groups could share with others.

The groups followed this pattern of reading, responding, and conferring for six to seven days. After completing the book, each group decided how to present some of their insights to the whole class. One group enacted skits of significant scenes, another "interviewed" characters, and a third created a collaborative sketch. These three group projects all contributed to the building of a supportive classroom community. Although only one of the projects involved a visual response to the story, all of the projects encouraged learners to take risks and to interpret texts in an aesthetic way.

5

In addition to the collaborative project, each individual student wrote a reaction paper about insights found while reading or while collaborating in the study group. The students could either write an essay or create a sketch and commentary. For this novel study we sent the essays to members of another class for written reflection after they had read the same novels. After completing the entire literary study, students wrote a reflection/evaluation of the experience (Figure 1–1). Derek's reflection/evaluation appears in Figure 1–2. [Note: All student work in italics appears in its unedited form.]

Students reflected on their growth ("In this study, I grew as a reader/writer/speaker/listener when . . ."). They also evaluated the structure of the study ("The best thing about this study/ "When we talked about our book, my group . . ."). Their insights helped me to reflect upon how to put my teaching beliefs into practice, and they guided our later studies by expressing their preferences for certain activities.

Figure 1–1. Reflection/Evaluation Form

1. When I was reading my book, I _____ .
2. When we talked about our book, my group _____ .
3. As I wrote in my response journal, I realized _____ .
4. I learned _____ .
5. I wish _____ .
6. The best thing about this study was _____ .
7. I would (or would not) like to read another book by the same author or about a similar subject _____ because _____ .
8. Ways that I grew as a reader/ writer/ speaker/ listener: _____ .
9. Our project _____ .
10. My individual paper _____ .

Figure 1–2. Derek's Reflection/Evaluation for *Summer of the Monkeys*

1. When I was reading my book, I *could picture the feelings of the different characters.*
2. When we talked about our book my group *discussed what they felt about the book so far.*
3. As I wrote in my response journal, I realized *different things I hadn't before.*
4. I learned *different ways to picture the book.*
5. I wish *the book Summer of the Monkeys wasn't so predictable.*
6. The best thing about this study was *being able to see the different ways my group pictured the book.*
7. I would like to read another book by the same author or about a similar subject. *Yes!* Because *he had good descriptions and a good way to get your attention.*
8. Ways I grew as a reader/writer/speaker/listener: *I grew as a listener because I learned different ways to picture the story.*
9. Our project *was fun to act out out as well as funny* (T.V. skit).
10. My individual paper *was a good experiance to have. I liked to draw out my different ideas.* [Derek's sketch and commentary appear in Figure 1–5.]

———

Throughout this study, sketching played an important role. Some students found sketching helpful in exploring ideas while reading; for others, sketching served as a vehicle for collaboration and as a synthesis of ideas. The stories behind the sketches showed me the importance of using pictures or symbols to make sense of stories. They also revealed the power of sketching to expand upon initial interpretations of those stories.

The Stories Behind the Sketching

Nathan and Troy spent the first few days of the study reading aloud to each other. During literature study time later in the week I found Troy leaning over his notebook sketching with colored pencils. Troy had drawn some hills, a wide river, and a tiny stick figure. Looming in the background was the outline of a chimpanzee's head (Figure 1–3). I looked on with interest.

"This is the big monkey," Nathan explained. "It's showing that whatever Jay Berry does, the big monkey is watching him." He further explained that Jay Berry could not get away with any trick to

Figure 1–3. Troy and Nathan's Sketch for *Summer of the Monkeys*

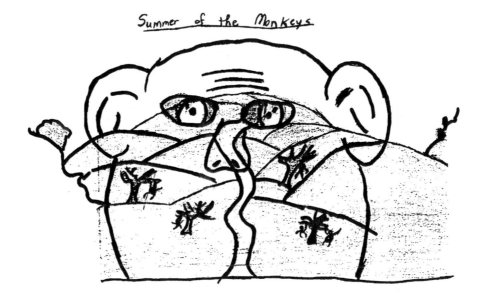

We tried to go into Jay Berrie's mind and figure out what he was thinking. This symbolizes what Jay Berry was thinking on the way back from the store with his traps. He'd be thinking about the river bottoms, then the 100 dollar monkey kept coming back to his mind.

capture the monkeys. I asked about the color of the eyes, which were reddish. "Red looks like it can see more," suggested Nathan.

"Yeah, and in the book when Jay Berry first saw the monkeys, he said the eyes looked red," added Troy.

"Oh, yeah, it did say that," remembered Nathan.

Together the boys had generated multiple meanings for the red eyes, one literal, one figurative. They had used the sketch to reflect upon their understandings of the main character's mind. When Troy sketched the chimpanzee, he exaggerated its size to convey Jay Berry's preoccupation with that animal.

Several weeks later I talked with Troy about this sketch and others. I asked him if he ever started a sketch but then changed it in the process of sketching. He turned to his co-authored monkey sketch and explained, "I was drawing, and we were going to put a bunch of trees and a bunch of monkeys, but it wasn't really the monkeys Jay Berry was talking about. It was more the big monkey, Jimbo." In this comment Troy showed me that authoring in art operates like authoring in writing. Troy had revised the plan he and Nathan had developed originally, that they should draw many monkeys in the trees.

I asked if the idea of Jimbo watching Jay Berry was partly his as well as Nathan's. Troy said yes, particularly the idea to make the eyes red, because red showed "penetrating eyes." Troy and Nathan both contributed to the sketch and its symbolic meaning. Through collaboration the boys were able to create something that they probably would not have created alone. As Troy looked at his sketch later, he further developed the ideas that the boys had generated by calling the all-seeing eyes "penetrating."

I also learned a great deal from a conversation with Melanie about a sketch that she made after she completed the book. She called her visual "Jay Berry's Block of Emotions" (Figure 1–4).

I was interested in the way she used punctuation marks to convey feelings. Since I wanted to know more about how she made her authoring decisions for this visual, I talked with her before school one day. I first asked Melanie general questions about how sketching helped her understanding. As she talked, she described her sketch

Figure 1–4. Jay Berry's block of emotions.

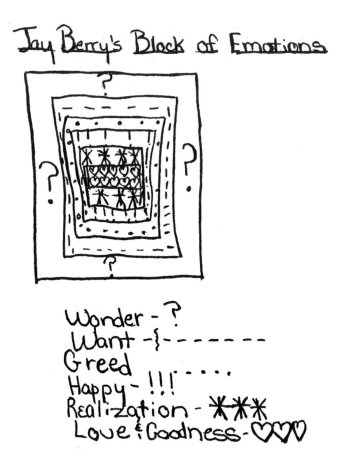

Jay Berry's Block of Emotions

Wonder - ?
Want - {- - - - - - -
Greed ! ! ! · · · ·
Happy - ! ! !
Realization - ✳✳✳
Love & Goodness - ♡♡♡

from "All Summer in a Day," which she called "Margot's Color Wheel of Emotions." In it she had used colors to show the changes in the main character's feelings.

I also asked, "Have you ever talked to someone and that made you change your sketch, or have you done them alone?" Melanie turned to the sketch (Figure 1–4) and said, "The Block of Emotions," and explained that she had recommended the book to her mom. When Melanie had showed her mom her sketch, Melanie's mother said that she thought "that Jay Berry also had greed about midway through the story." That idea inspired Melanie to revise her sketch. She reviewed her notes and decided where greed would fit into her draft, between "want" and "happy."

Melanie explained the rationale for her revised sketch to me in this way. "It's like the first part of the book, he just heard about the monkeys. He wondered about them. He didn't know if it was really true or anything. When he actually found out that it was true, he wanted to catch them 'cause he wanted the money. And then, as it went on he did different ideas and kinds of traps. And then he found out the monkeys were so much smarter. He got greedy for them, and he didn't stop anything to do it. So when he finally caught them he got happy about it, but then after he got the money, and he was picking out his pony, it just kind of dawned on him that he should give the money to Daisy. That was really what he had prayed for. And then his heart changed to love. His feelings kept changing, and I felt *Summer of the Monkeys* was an emotional book. The emotions and the feelings and the change cause it."

Our conversation helped her reflect upon her thought processes and put together the pieces of her thinking that led to her final sketch. As we continued to talk, I asked Melanie if someone else's sketch had ever caused her to think, "I could do one like that someday." Melanie replied, "That's where I kind of got the idea of the block. 'Cause at first I just thought it would have to be a wheel, and then Brandi had told me about a block of emotions, not really of emotions, but something that she'd done back in Mississippi, and that's when I kind of got the idea." Melanie's idea for the block did not come from a friend's sketch or even a book, but from an experience that her friend Brandi had outside of school. Melanie was drawing upon a wide range of experiences in her sketch: her own interpretation of the book, her conversations with her mom, her work with her literature circle in class, and her sharing of experiences with her best friend.

Finally, I wanted to ask Melanie more about the actual symbols in her sketch. I was still intrigued by her use of punctuation as a means to convey emotions. Melanie explained that, "You usually use punctuation marks to express the feelings for a sentence"—such as an exclamation point for happy. Turning to her sketch, she explained that to show Jay Berry's wonder she would naturally put question marks. "And, I thought like, when you want something, you just . . . it keeps going and going and going. . . . And then greed, that was just like in a book where it says dot, dot, dot, you're supposed to take it to mean more. He just eventually got greedy—the little dots [ellipses]. And realization. Like when you realize something and it dawns on you kind of like a flash of light. So I thought a star would be appropriate for that."

Melanie's story showed me another value of sketching one's understanding of a piece of literature. Melanie did not simply restate ideas by using language from the novel: she was forced to invent her own system of symbols to show her personal interpretation. She used both stylized artistic symbols, such as the heart and the star, as well as punctuation marks to convey her meaning. She thought about what punctuation marks do for a sentence: They add feelings, emotion, and expression. She showed how these same marks could be transformed to a new context to represent the emotions of a character. When I reflected upon the significance of Melanie's critical thinking, I better appreciated the concept of transmediation. *Transmediation* means expressing one's idea in a different communication system (in this case art and punctuation), from the system that the ideas were received (in this case a written novel). My conversation with Melanie showed me a value of sketching in interpreting literature. Teachers are often concerned that students may merely parrot back main ideas and supporting details of a story. Melanie's work showed that sketching helps readers move beyond the "who, what, when" of a story to personal interpretation through the process of transmediation. She described the book as "an emotional book." She had experienced the novel from the heart as she read it. Sketching enabled Melanie to explore the feelings behind the individual events

12

of the book and to keep from being reduced to summarizing the story and describing the characters.

Melanie's conversation challenged me as a teacher as well. It demonstrated to me how metaphor can link a concrete experience to an abstract concept. Elliot Eisner (1985, 1992) argues that all metaphors have their roots in physical sensation. Melanie had experienced the feelings of light illuminating darkness, so she easily sketched the star symbol to signify "realization," as the "light dawning."

My conversation with Melanie highlighted the value of metaphor in creating connections between learning events. An interest in metaphor grew over time as I talked with more students about visuals and as I read the work of other teacher-researchers. As a teacher I realized that the more I talked with students about their thinking, the more I wondered about the process of learning, and the more I wanted to know. As I tried to answer my wonderings, new questions and interests were born.

Sketching as an Avenue to Writing

Derek was stuck. His individual reaction paper to *Summer of the Monkeys* was due the next day, and as he told me later, he couldn't get his ideas straight. He decided to try a sketch-to-stretch because it could help him to express what he thought. He found that, "As I went on I thought of new ideas to put in my sketch-to-stretch." When he was finished with his sketch (Figure 1–5), he realized that through sketching he could express his feelings more easily.

When I talked with Derek about his authoring decisions, I realized that in creating the sketch several things happened. First, he was able to write a very detailed commentary for his sketch. Sketching had helped his writing. However, his writing conveys ideas in a different way from his sketch. One does not duplicate the other. Many other students have described sketches as a tool for "seeing the whole." Visual representations give an overall impression as well as specific details in a condensed way, or, as some students remarked "in a shorter

Figure 1–5. Derek's sketch for *Summer of the Monkeys*

My sketch-to-stretch shows the different emotions Jay Berry went through in Summer of the Monkeys.

First, Jay Berry was very happy and excited when his grandfather told him of the reward the circus was offering for the capture of the monkeys. I show this through the smiley face and the exclamation points.

Second, Jay Berry felt much hatred towards Jimbo whose intelligent actions prevented an easy capture of the monkeys. I show this through the colors red and black. The red represents hatred and the black represents Jay Berry's anger.

The blank box shows Jay Berry's frustration. The picture of Jimbo shows the source of Jay Berry's feelings.

The next section shows how Jay feels when he catches the two monkeys in the net. First, he is happy after catching the two monkeys. The next box shows the pain Jay experienced when he got bitten by the monkeys. The color yellow shows Jay Berry's unselfish feelings. He wishes to have Daisy's leg fixed.

The next section demonstrates Jay Berry's confidence building through a picture of a mountain. This is followed by different colors representing Jay Berry's sickness after drinking moonshine the monkeys tricked him into drinking. These colors are followed by the color brown which represents his feelings toward Daisy, who was trying to nurse him back to health against his wishes.

The next section shows Jay Berry's feelings when he catches the monkeys. First, it shows rain and the color black. The rain represents the storm and black shows fear of death or injury to the monkeys. It next shows the color white and exclamation points. The color white represents relief of the monkey's well being. The exclamation points represent excitement from catching the monkeys and being able to get the reward.

My final section shows what Jay Berry does with the money he receives for catching the monkeys. The first part shows a pony and a gun representing what Jay Berry wanted to buy with his reward. The smiley face and the exclamation point represent his excitement and happiness of getting the pony and gun. The next part shows Daisy, a question mark, and a dollar sign.

Daisy's crippled leg needs medical attention. Jay Berry wants to contribute his money towards Daisy's leg. This is what the dollar sign and Daisy represent. The question mark asks why Jay Berry had not wanted to give Daisy the money in the first place. The last part shows Daisy and Jay Berry in the center of the sun. If you notice, Daisy does not have her crutch. This picture represents Daisy after her operation. She is standing with Jay Berry in happiness. This concludes my sketch-to-stretch.

---

way." Secondly, although sketching was easier strategically than writing for Derek, his sketch shows sophisticated symbolism. Like Melanie, he did not simply restate ideas from the text; he invented his own symbol system. When I talked with him about his sketch, he described his process of constructing his own meaning as he invented a metaphorical symbol to convey his ideas. He pointed to the mountain, (fourth row, left), and said, "Well, if you see this mountain, what would you think? You wouldn't think it meant anything, just a mountain. But if you say like, it's courage climbing, then you can put a mountain. I mean like trying to reach the peak; it's courage building. When I was first thinking, I was thinking what could represent [that], I couldn't think of anything but a mountain, and I said, 'Well, that's a good idea.'"

Derek developed his idea for the mountain while he was sketching. As we were talking, he generated even more ideas for the meaning of another one of his symbols, the sun. He had originally meant the sun (bottom row, right) to stand for happiness, but as he described his ideas to me, he developed his ideas in new ways. He said, "The sun expresses happiness. Like, you don't think of the moon as sad, but, it's [the sun] like shining and bright; it's giving off life to plants, trees. That's not what I meant by this, but that just means what happens. It's like they were a piece of the sun, coming out. They were happy and joyful . . . it's a happy book."

Although Derek had decided to symbolize the happiness of the characters by placing them within the sun on his sketch, he had not thought of the detailed explanation for his choice until we talked together. During our conversation Derek extended his metaphor by associating the sun with its sustaining role for plants and animals. Jay Berry and Daisy were not merely superimposed on the sun, but they were figuratively part of it, sharing its energy: "Like they were a piece of the sun, coming out." His act of sketching had helped his writing, and our conversation encouraged his extended metaphor ("like a piece of the sun coming out . . ."). Even a finished sketch can be revised through collaborative talk.

Finally, Derek explained to me how he revised his ideas in his head before committing his thoughts to paper. This part of our conversation showed me that revision is a flexible process of thinking, not a formalized step of composing. I asked him if he had ever started drawing and then realized that the drawing could be different. Derek pointed to the present and explained, "I was just thinking that I could draw people, or something like that, but I said, 'Well, the present could represent something.' I was thinking which one showed my feelings more deeply. A present describes more feeling of giving."

In this portion of our conversation Derek helped me appreciate the role of revision. Revision is not necessarily a step that occurs after the creation of a rough draft. Instead, revision is the process of entertaining possibilities. Even before he committed a draft to paper, Derek had revised. He had considered a more literal interpretation of the story by showing a man giving Daisy the money, but he had wondered if that sketch would have conveyed the depth of the emotion that he felt from the event in the story. He decided that a present would symbolize the nature of giving more effectively. The act of giving was so important in the story that he placed the present in the middle of his sketch, even though that broke the chronological pattern he had established. Placement on the page, then, became an added symbol of significance. Reliving the text through this sketching had helped Derek consider deeply the feelings of the characters as well as his own feelings. The acts of reading, writing, drawing, and talking encouraged each other, yet each contributed a unique perspective to Derek's interpretation of the story.

Sketching Links Experiences

When Heather finished the novel, she created the following sketch (Figure 1–6).

Heather showed her friend Dahlia and me her sketch. We commented about her metaphor of Daisy as the sun, and Daisy's character trait of sensitivity to nature. Dahlia then remarked that Daisy didn't have a mouth. Heather considered Dahlia's idea, saying thoughtfully, "I hadn't put one in." Dahlia then suggested a new symbolic meaning —that Daisy kept the pain of her crippled leg and her feelings of loneliness to herself. Through our conversation the three of us saw new relationships in Daisy as a character. This new thought influenced a later experience of Heather.

17

Figure 1–6. Heather's sketch

The mountains are for where they lived.

The heart is Daisy. She was like the sun because she brightened every one's lives. She was a heart because she loved everything.

The eyes inside the heart means that you don't always have to see things with your eyes. You can see some things with your heart.

Maybe Daisy could see "The Man of the Mountains" with her heart.

A few months later Heather joined a literature circle that studied *Where the Lilies Bloom* (Cleaver and Cleaver 1969). After she completed the novel, she wrote the following response:

The visual I did for Summer of the Monkeys *can be used for this book too. The mountains stand for the Appalachian—where they lived. The sun is Mary Call. She is the head of the family, on the top like the sun. The reason she has no mouth is because she is holding her hurt and I think a little anger. The hurt is for Roy Luther—his death. The anger is for Roy Luther too. He had left her in charge. She was fourteen and forced to become an adult. The eyes are for seeing in the future. She was head of the house and had to make plans for her family.*

I was excited when Heather wrote this response. Again I saw the value of informal conversation. Dahlia and Heather generated new ideas by talking informally about Heather's sketch. Heather did not consider leaving the mouth out as "wrong," but rather as an invitation to explore new ideas. We had built a spirit of inquiry and risk-taking in the classroom; Heather did not feel threatened by this conversation. Instead, she built upon the idea in a later reader's response as she reflected upon *Where the Lilies Bloom*. It was also important that Heather used her understanding of one text in order to make sense of another. Her sketch served as a framework to compare themes, conflict, and character traits of two entirely different novels. My thinking about Heather's comments strengthened my belief that making connections between experiences is a crucial part of learning.

Heather had an additional opportunity to reflect upon these connections when she selected entries for her portfolio. Students collected several samples of personally significant work each grading period to place in a portfolio. Heather chose her second sketch and essay for her portfolio, and her accompanying commentary showed her perception of her learning through sketching.

I have made a connection between Daisy and Mary Call. (The visual I did, helped with this connection). I chose this because it shows what visuals can do. I think visuals are powerful and help to see things in different ways.

This experience with sketching helped Heather become an empowered learner. She knew herself well as a learner. She knew that she could use sketching to help create mental connections between characters across texts. She understood that by conversing with peers and adults, she could generate ideas that extended her own original thoughts, and she could continue to build upon those ideas over time. Understanding her own strategies for learning helped Heather be an active inquirer through experiences with literature and through tying together those experiences.

Sharing Sketches Generates New Ideas

Abby, Doug, Brent, and Rachel worked together in a study group. For their final presentation they decided to construct a large sketch representing the entire novel. Since the poster was big, I have sketched a reduced version in Figure 1–7. They revised their ideas as they constructed the poster, but what is significant for our purposes here is their sharing of their visual representation with the whole class.

As the group displayed the poster for the class to see, they each contributed to the explanation of its symbolism. I have combined their statements here:

> This is our sketch-to-stretch. The heart represents [Jay Berry's] thoughts and what he sees. And the line represents the before, and this (points below the line) is after. This whole heart with the little broken line here, it represents Jay Berry and the monkeys aren't really good friends. And the little girl who has the deformed leg is Daisy because she has a crippled leg. And that little thing like a leg-trapper thing represents him trying to catch the monkeys. And this part is like later on, the Band-Aid (a real one) on the heart 'cause they're happy. And that's Jimbo. And that's the monkey and Daisy after she got her new leg. And the arrow shows before and after and then the little horse and the gun. That's what he got, like his reward for catching the monkeys and everything. And these are all the characters (on the side on the line). Grandpa, Grandma, Dad, Mom, Jay Berry, and Daisy, and Rowdy. And you

Figure 1–7. Collaborative sketch

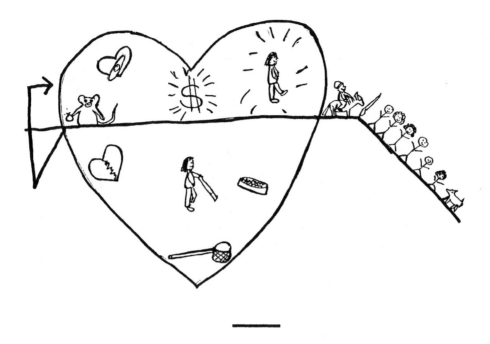

turn the page so you can see them. Like if they're upside down, you turn it, and like turning the page symbolizes them turning around in their life.

Several class members commented on the sketch. Troy liked the Band-Aid. He said, "At first [Jay Berry] had a broken heart, and the monkeys fixed it for him." I was interested in Troy's remark because the members of the group had not specifically said that the monkeys fixed Jay Berry's broken heart. I saw that the close placement of the monkey to the heart could be further support for Troy's idea, and I acknowledged Troy as the inspiration for this connection. Then Nathan thought of still another idea. He remarked, "I can help him out, too. 'Cause like, when [Jay Berry] was trying to catch the monkey, he was all frustrated. He kind of had a broken heart because he was trying as hard as he could. And then when he finally did catch them he was like, on top of the world." Nathan strengthened Troy's idea by showing that Jay Berry's heart might have been broken by frustration, and this heart was mended when he caught the monkeys. Both boys had added new ideas to the interpretation of the original sketch through collaborative discussion.

As the group concluded their presentation Rachel, one of the authors, studied the poster once more and mused, "We should have done the fairy ring." (The characters in the story made wishes while sitting in a legendary ring of mushrooms.)

I responded by asking, "Where would you put the fairy ring?" Several children contributed ideas, saying "around the heart," "around Daisy," "instead of the sunshine . . . they could put Daisy there . . ." Then Nathan broke in, "Hey listen . . . they could have put the fairy ring like in the middle of the 'after' part. In the very middle, kind of everything revolves around it."

Troy spoke next, "I was going to say it could go all around, like all the way around everything." After a few more minutes of discussion, I realized that our conversation was demonstrating an important point. The group had presented their poster as a final draft, yet we were brainstorming mental revisions as if it were a rough draft. Our discussion was showing that a draft is never truly finished; instead, a draft or a text should be alive and changing as it is shared with different audiences. Texts are not sacred. They exist so that both authors and receivers can use them to make sense of their experiences. I had expected the sharing session to be a presentation, but instead it had become a reflective discussion about what it means to be authors of ideas.

As I thought about this day over time, I realized the important role that a spirit of community plays in generating new meanings. When the group first presented their poster to the class, they viewed it as a final draft. Rachel took a risk in voicing the opinion that she and her group might have included the fairy ring. Instead of seeing their omission as a mistake, Rachel's group welcomed the contributions of the class as different members offered alternative interpretations. Although many members of the class may have kept their original opinions for the placement of the fairy ring, the multiple interpretations generated by the class added depth to everyone's understanding.

The conversation also showed me that listening and viewing are active processes of constructing meaning. Troy did not help sketch the poster, but by looking at the heart with the Band-Aid, he thought of Jay Berry's relationship to the monkeys in a new way. Nathan's commanding conclusion that "everything revolves around" the fairy ring also shows active construction of meaning through listening and viewing. Nathan was not an author of the poster but generated new insights for its interpretation.

Finally, this conversation caused me to reflect upon my role as a teacher. I showed that I was a learner who benefited from conversation by telling Troy that his idea about the Band-Aid was new to me. On the other hand, my question, "Did you do that on purpose?" showed that I took the opportunity to raise students' awareness of intentionality. I invited alternative meanings, such as when I asked the group where they might put the fairy ring. I encouraged the group to take a reflective stance on the nature of literacy by discussing our revision of a final draft. This conversation helped to build an environment in which we all valued multiple interpretations and we all reflected upon how learners come to know. This sharing session supported us to create a community where process was more important than product, and where inquiry was more important than certainty.

Looking Back over the Literature Study

When I reflected upon the events of the entire novel study, I saw several key features of sketching. Melanie and Derek (Figures 1–4, 1–5) showed me that there is no one-to-one correspondence between a text and a set of symbols to represent it. As a class we were learning to appreciate the varied perspectives that each sketch provided. We were also coming to see that sketching generated new ideas that were impossible to show through language. Although writing supports drawing and drawing supports writing, each system contributes unique ideas and a unique perspective.

This literary study gave me an appreciation for the huge invest-ment of mental energy necessary for the creation of visual symbols to convey ideas, and the potential of re-using those symbols in a variety of contexts. I could see that when given the opportunity to sketch regularly, learners begin to search through their personal "storehouses" of sketches for past symbols to re-use. For example, when Heather thought about *Where the Lilies Bloom*, she remembered her sketch for *Summer of the Monkeys*. She used the visual symbols that she had already created as a lens to view her latest reading experience. In this way, she was able to connect two entirely differ-ent novels, thus strengthening her understanding of the theme of independence and courage.

Finally, this experience showed me the importance of cultivating a spirit of inquiry in a learning community. Learners used sketching as a vehicle to explore ideas rather than to accept the author's draft as "final." Flexible thinking in these discussions encouraged risk-taking in the group. Learners came to value the creation of new ideas through the contributions of many voices. The study of *Summer of the Monkeys* set the tone for our classroom community for the rest of the year.

TWO

Sketching and the Authoring Cycle

So I'm saying that when you're in an authors' circle for visuals, you get ideas, and you revise it (your visual) just like a writer.

SETH, *Grade 7*

It was late April, and Seth was discussing with three classmates how they went about sketching in response to reading. Seth's comment startled me. Here a thirteen-year-old was drawing parallels between sketching and writing in a simple, straightforward way. He realized that as he discussed his sketches with his peers and with me, he generated new ideas and revised his thinking in ways that were similar to his work in Writers' Workshop. As a teacher and a researcher, I had spent countless hours reading and discussing with colleagues theory that linked processes of authoring across systems of communication. Seth's experiences and opportunity to reflect upon these experiences had led him to draw similar conclusions. Seth's poignant analysis of the process of sketching helped me relate research to classroom practice and to listen even more closely to students' explanations of their thinking.

The Authoring Cycle Model

I have found Harste, Short and Burke's authoring cycle model (1988) a helpful tool to think about the process of creating. These authors represented their ideas as a cycle to emphasize the way in which ideas and strategies build upon each other over time. The model emphasizes the role of social relationships in creating in several ways. First, life experiences serve as foundations for learners to build understanding. For example, a child reading a book relates to a character who is nervous about the first day of school because the reader has had similar feelings. Secondly, as learners discuss ideas developed from reading, writing, sketching, and so on, they revise their thinking by considering the perspectives of others. Finally, as learners observe the work of peers and published authors, they find opportunities to borrow one another's strategies for expressing ideas, such as beginning a piece of writing with a quotation to develop the interest of the audience. As I explored the process of sketching with my students, I found parallels that were anchored in the same base of social interaction. Seth's comment confirmed this relationship for me. I examined children's work from the year with this framework in mind, and I was able to value sketching in a new way after this experience.

Life Experiences as the Foundation for Sketching

I knew that authors draw upon what they know best as they write. What did this idea mean for sketching? I started to watch for examples of ties that students made between their personal experiences and their sketching. One day Adam related to me how he used ideas from his experiences outside the classroom to create sketches. We were looking through his journal and discussing sketches. Two sketches, which he selected for his portfolio, demonstrated the connections he made between his experiences at home and his reading. One was a mouse in a maze that he had used to symbolize a murder mystery, and the other was a sketch of two magnets (Figure 2–1).

Figure 2–1. Adam's sketches

a. A mouse in a maze to represent how confused Shari was about her death.

b. The two magnets represent how great Redruth and Squire's friendship really was. The Squire feels guilty that the bullet didn't hit him.

Looking at the maze, Adam explained that he used a lot of animal-related ideas in his sketches because animals were important to him. "I mean, I've caught fish (a subject of another sketch), and (at home) I have a hamster in a cage with a lot of pipes. The hamster has a connection with this one. I thought of that (the pipes), and I thought, well, maybe a maze, 'cause I can't draw pipes." I was intrigued as I pictured Adam at home with his reader's response journal before him. I could imagine him looking around his room while he thought about the confusion in the mystery. The hamster cage caught his eye, and he connected the mazelike pipes with the suspense, twists, and turns in the mystery. Realizing that the cage was difficult to draw, he searched mentally for an easier object to sketch, and he thought of a mouse in a maze. He checked his new idea against the feeling in the book, and finding it consistent, he took his pencil and created his sketch.

I wanted to know more about Adam's perspective on gleaning his ideas from home, so I asked him if he could describe any of his thinking as he made these types of connections. He answered, "I just think of something like, [if] I sat on my dock and I saw a water moccasin, if I have a reader's response the next day, that's what I'll do it on. And I won't have a choice. I can't just say 'No' and not do it. I have to do it. I guess it has to do with me. I just can't leave stuff there."

Adam's statement that he "can't just leave stuff there" showed me that authors of sketches, like authors of writing, use their personal life experiences as a base to construct meaning. Adam created metaphors that were meaningful to him, and those metaphors helped him make connections between his personal life and his understanding of his reading. Reading, thinking about reading, and expressing his thoughts about reading through his sketches were all dependent on his own environment.

Turning to his sketch of the magnets (Figure 2–1b), Adam showed me how he created in his head before he put his pen to paper. Again he had a reader's response for homework, and as he prepared to work, he became hungry. His mind wandered to the refrigerator. He said, "I thought of the refrigerator, and then I thought of the refrigerator door, and of those magnets you stick on it. And I thought of the refrigerator being one magnet, and the food sticking to it, like they were best friends. And so I just drew two magnets. I thought, 'Well, Squire and Redruth are like two magnets too, so I can draw Squire and Redruth as two magnets, 'cause the refrigerator and the food were two magnets, and they're best friends."

Adam constructed a unique interpretation of the character relationship because he drew upon his personal view of his world (hunger) as he reflected upon his reading. He used a familiar object in his house, the refrigerator, as a reference point for his experience with reading. Just as the maze metaphorically represented confusion to Adam, the relationship of a refrigerator door and a magnet represented friendship. By linking two seemingly unrelated experiences, Adam constructed new meaning for himself. His personal understanding of the text grew through his sketching. Later he shared this sketch with students and with me, and the larger group benefited from his perspective. I could see that each of our personal experiences, brought into the classroom through sketching, generated multiple views of our common reading. In this way our understanding could be enriched in new ways. Through this conversation with Adam, I came to appreciate the relationship between the growth of each learner as an individual and as a member of a group.

Not only did I listen more closely to students like Adam about the relationship between their experiences and their sketching, but I also began to reflect more deeply upon my own process of sketching. A series of my own experiences showed me clearly how life experiences can change an interpretation of the same text over time. For several years I read aloud Martin Luther King Jr.'s "I Have a Dream" speech to the class, and we created collaborative sketches, posters, or collages as a response. My sketch each year varied as I focused upon different images, and as I learned from my students through their sharing. On one occasion I led a group of adults through the experience while at a conference at Niagara Falls. Earlier in the day I had visited the Falls, listening to the roar of the rushing water, its enormous energy, and gazing upon the rainbow that hovered in the mists of the waterfall. Later, as I read the part of the speech that includes the analogy of "justice rolling down like waters," the image of the water's power and the rainbow's symbol of hope from my experience at the Falls flashed in my mind. The morning's experience deepened my appreciation of the beliefs in the power of good and of justice in the speech. Despite the fact that I had read King's speech many times, I gained a fresh perspective and new insights as an author of ideas that day. This experience demonstrated to me vividly that creating draws upon experiences, and new experiences contribute to the creation of ideas. I knew in a fresh way that a text is not stagnant nor fixed, but instead, it is a potential that grows with meaning over time. I also realized that it is not enough for teacher-researchers to observe other learners and to ask them about their thinking; we need to participate in the process ourselves. Through my own personal perspective I could better share my new insights about the speech and about the process of creating with my students and colleagues.

Finding Surprise and Discovery Through Sketching

Adam, his classmates, and I found that we generated new ideas in the process of sketching. Similarly, in writing Donald Murray (1968) asserts that we do not write to record what we know, but to discover what we did not know. Reflecting upon the work of students allowed me to pursue this feature of generating new ideas in sketching. I asked many students what went through their heads as they sketched. Derek showed in his sketch of *Summer of the Monkeys* (Figure 1-5) that sketching helped him make new connections and that the process of drawing enabled him to convey his ideas in written form as well. Derek sketched because he was "stuck," and he became "unstuck" as he discovered meaning through sketching.

I was surprised, however, by my talk with another student, Heidi, about her process of discovery through uninterrupted sketching. Heidi was one of the most accomplished writers in the class, so I doubted that she would use sketching to lead the way to writing as Derek had done. Moreover, she did not feel particularly competent as an artist. She had changed a character in a children's book that she wrote from a cow to a sheep because she didn't think she could draw cows well enough for the illustrations. For these reasons I was surprised by a portfolio commentary Heidi wrote about her sketch of *Where the Lilies Bloom*. The sketch and portfolio commentary appear in Figure 2–2.

When I read this entry, I was eager to talk with Heidi. I wanted to know more about her feelings toward this visual and what it did for her as a learner. I was particularly intrigued by her comment that this sketch was "The kind I had been wanting to do all year." Obviously, she saw a potential in sketching that she did not see in writing. I decided to ask her what drawing did for her that writing could not do. She answered, "You can see the people, where they are, and it kind of organizes it because you can see just by looking what things are where. And you don't have to follow through in a paragraph, like when you're trying to describe something, instead of using phrases, everybody sees it."

Figure 2–2. Heidi's sketch

The wavy line is an uplifted chin—that's Luther's pride. They do not accept help from others—they bury Roy Luther privately, the way he wanted it (the mound and shovel). And, so represented by the sapling, rose, and plant inside the rim of the basket, they wildcraft to earn a living. Even when the roof is caving in under the weight of the snow, the children sustain themselves. However—outside the chin—they do accept some "help"—Kiser's car, and the pig and cow.

Roughly drawn in the background are the Luther children: Mary Call, staunchly against outside help, Romey, Ima Dean, and lastly Devola, willing to accept help from others, especially Kiser.

Portfolio entry: I chose this Reader's Response sketch-to-stretch because I thought it held a lot of meaning. It was the kind of sketch-to-stretch I had been wanting to do all year but couldn't. Then I came up with the chin idea, etc. It is one of my favorite sketch-to-stretches because it sums up the themes of the book and this pride that holds the Luthers together.

Her explanation brought to mind a comment Seth had made that sketches are "a shorter way" to show an author's meaning. Troy had said that, "You get more out of it [sketch] just by looking at it and drawing it. Kind of like a graph." Malti had cited the old saying, "A picture is worth a thousand words." Even though Heidi wrote easily and well, she saw a unique potential of communication in creating her sketch. I began to sense that the students were showing me that sketches condensed ideas while blending both cognitive and affective dimensions of a piece of literature. When a person looks at a sketch, one sees an integrated whole, a gestalt. Feelings and images merge. There is no linear progression. Visual representations hold a unique potential for conveying meaning.

When I asked Heidi about the thinking behind her portfolio comment, her answer revealed additional potential of artistic representation as a communication system: "I never thought my sketch-to-stretches were good. And then, I was getting ready to go in the shower, and I thought, 'What am I going to do?' And all of a sudden I realized that I could do, [something] like this [Heidi pointed to the chin on her sketch]. And after that I decided I could put these on one side or the other [small figures]. And then the people kind of landed here. It just happened, that they were that way, and then I thought that's like the way they were put in the story. I didn't plan it that way; it just happened. Oh, I wanted to draw specific characters in the book. And, they're the ones that are proud and all . . . I was just drawing Mary Call, and I realized that that was where they had fallen. And where the people had fallen had a match to their characters, their personalities."

Heidi showed me that although sketching had a potential that writing did not (showing the relationship of parts to a whole in one glance), the process of mulling over possibilities in one's head is similar in both writing and sketching. Donald Graves says that learners who have regular opportunities to write, compose mentally even when they are not writing on paper (1983). Heidi's comments and those of her classmates showed that these students were sketching in their heads in the same way. Heidi and many other students indicated that an idea for a sketch just "came," but when they described their process of thinking, it became clear that the image "coming" was not an isolated event. Heidi was mentally constructing, abandoning, and revising images in her mind as she prepared to shower. Although she said that her idea "just came," her image of a chin was the result of a long process of creating texts mentally. She was sketching in her head in a similar way that writers compose in their heads.

In our conversation Heidi gave another reason for choosing the sketch as one of her best pieces of work. She explained that some of her earlier sketches had been simple illustrations of a story. These illustrations did not need long commentaries because there was little symbolism to explain. Heidi remarked, "Sometimes I draw some part of the story. [A picture] doesn't need a long commentary. It doesn't represent anything." It was the symbolic quality of this sketch that led Heidi to categorize her portfolio sketch as one of her best. She had thought hard about the meaning of the story and then created a new set of symbols to express her knowing visually. She felt that the *Lilies* sketch was different from an illustration. Sketches have different purposes just as different genres of writing have different purposes.

Finally, Heidi's conversation showed me another important feature of creating sketches. I was surprised when she said that she did not mean to place her figures in the way that she did, that they "had landed here . . . and where the people had fallen had a match to their personalities." In the process of creating, Heidi generated new meanings. When she remained open to the element of surprise, she began to look for more and more purpose in the elements of placement and proximity. She looked to her sketch as a vehicle to generate more ideas. In doing so, she reflected upon the character relationships in the book and deepened her understanding of the whole. Her initial image, the chin to represent the pride of the characters, was based upon her understanding of the book. The characters "landed here," and she mentally searched the meanings that she had created for the text in a new light. The act of committing her initial ideas on paper helped her learn more from her reading. The process of creating, both in writing and sketching, helps learners to discover and generate new meanings about experiences.

Reflecting and Revising in Sketching

Discovering and generating meaning becomes even more powerful when learners share ideas with each other. The authoring cycle model emphasizes the role of making sense of our experience with the social support of others. In Chapter 1 the story of the collaborative visual of *Summer of the Monkeys* and Melanie's discussion of "Jay Berry's Block of Emotions" show the importance of exploring ideas in a group. Through such conversations members of the class developed more flexible thinking and began to look at literature from fresh perspectives. I, too, learned to be a more flexible thinker from participating in group discussions and talking with individual students in the months that followed.

In the following fall Rebekah and her classmates showed me an additional dimension about the part that conversation plays in revision, reflection, and extension of ideas. Rebekah had read the novel *Lyddie* (Paterson 1991) and sketched Figure 2–3.

Several of her classmates had previously sketched what the class called "character hearts," a heart with symbols signifying character traits and interests, but Rebekah's looked different. She had included a wide band of yellow outlining the entire heart. Before class Rebekah showed me her visual. We talked about it for a few minutes. During our conversation I questioned her about the yellow band, and she told me that she had not meant it to "mean anything." I asked her for permission to show the class her sketch before she explained her own decisions as an author so that we could see what ideas the class might have about the band (See Chapter 1, "Save the Last Word for Me" strategy). She agreed.

When Rebekah displayed her sketch to the class, several of her peers contributed ideas about the meaning of the yellow band. Julia, who had also read *Lyddie*, suggested that the band could show that Lyddie had a warm heart even though she seemed mean on the outside. Andrea said, "Every cloud has a silver lining," indicating that goodness and hope emerged through the tears and sadness of the circumstances of the plot. Looking at the heart thoughtfully, Rebekah mused that the yellow could mean that Lyddie hid her heart from

Figure 2–3. Rebekah's sketch

people, and the yellow could represent a barrier. Rebekah's comment inspired Lindsay to compare the band to a turtle's shell since Lyddie "wrapped her heart up." Jennifer added that the yellow might show that Lyddie was strong and powerful at the end of the story since yellow is a bold and bright color.

Then Robert spoke. Robert had not read the story, so I was particularly interested in his response. He suggested that the yellow band reminded him of the yellow ribbons that people displayed as symbols of coming home during the Persian Gulf War. The girls who had read the story nodded, "Yeah!" One of them justified Robert's comment by explaining to the whole class that during the major part of the book Lyddie endeavored to save money so that she could prevent her Vermont farm from being sold. All of her trials in the story centered around her desire to return to her beloved cabin. The yellow ribbon from the Persian Gulf War that Robert mentioned gave Rebekah and the members of her literature circle the opportunity to make this new connection with Lyddie and her desire to return to her home.

These insights that we generated during the discussion were exciting for several reasons. First, Rebekah had expanded the meaning of her draft by conversing with others. Originally she did not have a meaning for the yellow band, but as her friends contributed their ideas, she realized that it could illustrate an important part of Lyddie's character. Secondly, the entire class thought flexibly about the symbol and about the interpretation of the text. We were entertaining possibilities of meaning generated by these multiple perspectives. We built ideas upon each other, such as the barrier leading to the idea of a turtle's shell, but each idea provided a unique perspective on the events and main character of the book. Third, we were encouraged to return to the text for justification of ideas. For example, Jennifer used the yellow band to highlight Lyddie's confidence in taking charge of her own future at the end of the story. Finally, Robert's comment illustrated an important feature of the authoring cycle model to me, that listening and viewing are constructive acts. Robert had not read this book, but by viewing Rebekah's sketch and by listening to the conversation of his classmates, he generated a logical idea that inspired further reflection on the part of the girls who had studied the novel. When Robert associated the Persian Gulf War to the color of yellow, he also illustrated that we draw upon our life experiences as we construct meaning. As we closed our discussion, I pointed out the significance of Robert's comment from the point of an author constructing meaning through listening. I wanted the students to reflect not only upon the literary elements of the novel, but upon the value of constructing meaning as a group. Whether or not members of a group have experienced exactly the same text, then, they can contribute insights that encourage authors to reflect upon their ideas and to revise them.

Considering the Audience in Sketching

A key feature of the authoring cycle is publishing. Publishing heightens the importance of two issues in writing: the concept of audience and the use of conventions or rules of format. These issues are closely related, and working with sketching helped me to understand and to value their role in communication both in writing and in drawing. As I learned more, I encouraged students to reflect on these connections as well.

Graves (1983) and others have discussed the shift in writers' perspectives as they become more aware of the needs of an audience. By sharing drafts in authors' circles, writers come to anticipate the questions, "What did you mean by . . . ?," "I am confused about . . . ." or "Could you tell me more about . . . ?" As authors internalize these questions, they revise in order to clarify and expand their ideas while composing initial drafts. They come to know themselves as authors as well as the audiences with whom they are most familiar, and they plan authoring strategies based on this knowledge.

I found similar processes occurring as groups became more and more familiar with sketching. Seth taught me one of my first lessons about the role of audience in creating visually. He was working with Samantha and Malti in a literary study of *All Together Now*. One day in September he showed his group a sketch he had created the day before (Figure 2–4), which showed the relationship between two characters. He used red to symbolize love, blue to represent hope, and black for a rift in their relationship. Seth explained that from left to right the red stood for the two getting married, the blue for the woman's hope, the black for divorce, the second blue for the man's hope, and the red the "getting back together."

The three argued over a few of the events in the book that led to his choice of colors, and Malti suggested changing one color to

Figure 2–4. Seth's sketch of relationships in *All Together Now*

red	light blue	black	dark blue	red	

———

yellow. A few minutes later I came by and asked, "Is there some reason why this blue is lighter and this is darker?" Seth replied, "I didn't . . ." when Malti interrupted with, "Yeah."

Seth was amazed. "There is?"

Malti answered, "Yeah. Hazard's hope is different."

Seth considered his sketch again. "Oh, yeah. Hazard's hope is stronger than Pansy's hope, 'cause she had already filed for divorce."

Seth revised his ideas about the two colors of blue while talking with Malti and me. I had raised the question about his intentions behind the two shades. Although he had not differentiated them in his mind while sketching, Malti offered a possible meaning as she considered my question. Seth then confirmed her suggestion, as Rebekah had confirmed Robert's yellow ribbon idea for Figure 2–3. Seth's conversation influenced his understanding of communicating with a specific audience.

A few weeks later Seth decided to put his revised sketch in his portfolio as an example of a significant piece showing his growth. In the final draft he had differentiated between the two shades of blue, saying that "the light blue is to symbolize hope for Pansy, the dark blue is for Hazard's hope." We talked about his choice to include this piece in his portfolio. He acknowledged his classmates' influence in his process of sketching. He said, "Samantha and Malti really helped it. They really changed it. Because after I showed them this (draft), they put a lot of input in. I don't think I really did intend to have the light blue and dark blue, but then I think Malti pointed it out, and I just thought, 'Well, yeah, I intended that . . . that's a good idea.'"

The conversation about color had influenced Seth's composition in another way as well. As he prepared to place the sketch in his portfolio, he shifted his thinking to his anticipation of the girls' reaction to his commentary. He told me, "When I was writing my description, I also added something in my description that I thought about this last night . . . that the rectangle symbolized Hazard and Pansy. It symbolized both of them, and this (the blocks of color) is inside their marriage. This is their feelings." I looked again at his commentary, and I noticed that indeed he had begun this revised draft with, "This is to symbolize Hazard and Pansy." Seth continued to explain why he had added this dimension. "While I was fixing my portfolio last night, I was reading over my paper [an accompanying essay]. Well, after I read my paper I looked at it [the sketch], I just thought, 'Now if this is going to be a pattern, then the rectangle has to mean something.' I mean, people are going to ask, 'Why did you choose a rectangle instead of a circle or a triangle?' I just figured to say that the rectangle was just their feelings."

Seth's explanation of his thinking shows the value of sharing one's writing or drawing with others. Seth read and responded to his reading through writing and sketching. Through sharing with his peers and me, Seth considered other perspectives about his piece. He changed his strategies by anticipating an outside audience's reaction to his revised draft. Social interaction changed Seth as a learner. Just as an author of writing learns to consider the perspective of an audience, Seth sketched in a different way as he shifted his thinking from his own thoughts to the reactions of his peers.

Seth's story also helped me understand a second issue of publishing, the function of conventions or rules in communication. I began to appreciate more deeply that conventions arise from the need to share similar meanings within social groups. Seth's conversation with Samantha and Malti paved the way for all of them to share an understanding that shades of color conveyed specific meanings. In writing I knew that punctuation in written language, for example, encouraged communication of an author's intended meaning. Writing done for personal purposes, such as shopping lists, could be abbreviated, misspelled, or coded in a way that only the author could understand. However, as authors share with wider and wider audiences, conventions serve to convey the author's intentions. Commas, semicolons, and periods help to group thoughts. Quotation marks indicate word-for-word dialogue, and separate paragraphs for new quotes help readers keep track of the speakers. I came to understand this function of shared conventions more clearly through our explorations with sketches. Various classes (or groups of classes in different academic years) developed unique rules of expression which helped their specific groups. These conventions arose from a need to make intentions clear within the group.

Sometimes class members benefit from another's use of a symbol even though they do not actually use it in their sketches. I learned this important lesson about conventions from a student in Heidi's class, Jacob. Jacob invented his own way to represent a character's feelings. His symbol, distorted arrows, showed confusion. Although he used his symbol over time as he read different books, others in the class did not follow his lead. However, the comments of students showed me that Jacob's tool was accepted as a convention by his class.

Jacob first used distorted arrows to show internal conflict in the novel *Roll of Thunder, Hear My Cry* (Taylor 1977), (Figure 2–5). When I asked him about his symbol, he explained that arrows show confusion because "You don't know which way to go."

Figure 2–5. Jacob's sketch

This shows the confusion Cassie is going through. All that she's heard and what she's seen is confusing to her.

Jacob read *Homecoming* (Voigt 1981) in December. This time he extended his idea. In this representation, the intensity of internal conflict was highlighted because now Jacob placed the arrows inside the character's head (Figure 2–6).

In February Jacob expanded upon his arrow theme once again. This time he was reading *Treasure Island* (Stevenson 1895, 1981). Jacob added a knife to signify Jim's fear (Figure 2–7).

Although I photocopied and shared Jacob's visuals with his class, other students did not choose to use his strategy of using arrows to signify confusion and internal conflict. However, the members of the class recognized Jacob as "the arrow person." Jill, for example, commented during a discussion that she had seen Jacob's arrows "a million times," and that he used "his little man." Jacob's strategy enabled him to have conversations with his classmates; they shared an understanding of his meaning. Knowing that Jacob's arrows meant confusion allowed Jacob and his audience to communicate with each other. The convention or rule conserved the energy of the

Figure 2–6. Jacob's sketch

This shows Dicey's confusion and sadness. She is confused about her mom. She is sad because she thinks her mom left her.

Figure 2–7. Jacob's sketch

This shows Jim's feelings. He is afraid which is represented by the knife, and he is confused which is represented by the arrows.

---

group because they did not have to ask Jacob to explain everything about his sketch each time he used arrows. Learners can appreciate the meanings of others even though they do not use certain symbols or conventions actively. We know more conventions than we use. In language use, members of a culture or community are aware of a wider choice of idioms, expressions, or dialects than they choose to include in their own speech or writing. In sketching, Jacob's classmates did not use his arrow symbol, but they shared an understanding of its meaning when he presented his drafts to a group. Creating and using conventions for the purpose of sharing meaning with audiences, then, is similar in both writing and sketching.

Sharing and Reflecting—an Invitation to Others

In the authoring cycle, learners take time to reflect upon the strategies of peer and published authors. These discussions highlight opportunities for individuals to explore in future writing experiences. Studying how authors create effective leads is an example of a strategy lesson in a writing classroom. Similarly, as authors of sketches examine their own work and the work of their classmates, they develop a repertoire of strategies to explore. After my experience with the literary study of *Summer of the Monkeys*, I became more sensitive to the importance of devoting chunks of time to reflect upon sketching strategies as a group. The next fall I was determined to emphasize strategy sharing from the very first experience with sketching. Reflecting upon the sketches for "All Summer in a Day" in one class inspired a yearlong invitation for sketching.

Both the students and I marveled at Jennifer's interpretation of the story, Figure 2–8.

The large, bold, stylized shapes around the heart were darkened with black ink. The heart that represented Margot, the only character who had seen the sun, was vibrant with the green, yellow, blue, and white colors of a landscape and sky. Jennifer outlined the heart with a slender band of red. We spent several minutes in class discussing Jennifer's sketch and asking her about her process of creating it. This conversation was the foundation for future experiences throughout the year.

Within a few weeks, Erin built upon Jennifer's idea of representing the feelings of a character by sketching a heart. However, Erin sketched two hearts that contrasted the main character's feelings at the beginning of the book with the feelings at the end of the story. When Erin shared her drawings with the class, she credited Jennifer as her inspiration. This conversation helped to establish the idea of "character hearts" as a shared symbol in the class. Many of Jennifer's classmates developed variations of the character heart theme during the fall and winter. Rebekah's character heart of *Lyddie*, Figure 2–3, was one of the sketches from this particular class.

Months later another sketch by Jennifer provided the class with a new strategy to explore. Jennifer sketched Figure 2–9 after completing the chapter in *Treasure Island* when Jim discovers Long John Silver's plot to overthrow the captain of the ship. Jim, of course, had trusted Long John Silver completely up until this point.

Figure 2–8. Jennifer's sketch

In my picture I explained what I thought the meaning of the story meant. To me the sun, blue skies, flowers, and green grass was Margot's heart. And the rain, dead grass, and other dead objects represent the children's hearts. I'm also saying Margot has a wonderful memory of what life is all about that the other children will never have.

P.S. It's hard for me to explain everything my picture means because it's so very complicated.

Figure 2–9. Jennifer's sketch

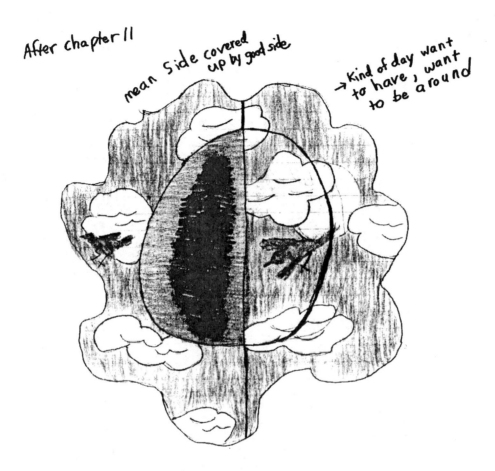

This represents Long John. The sky represents Long John's good side. The dark scribbles represent Long John's bad side, but it is covered up by a fake good side.

———

As was our custom, Jennifer shared her sketch with her literature circle and later with the whole class. We spent part of the class period discussing the strategies that she used in her sketch. During our reading of the novel, we had been fascinated with Long John Silver as a character, and Jennifer's sketch enabled us to examine him from a new perspective. The sketch enriched our understanding of the way in which Long John deceived those around him by putting up a front. Since he changed his personality as he interacted with different people, his true feelings remained a mystery. Jennifer's classmates felt that the clouds that obscured parts of the sky helped to convey his ambiguous nature.

Erin combined the ideas from both the clouds sketch and the character heart theme, but she added an extended metaphor that enabled her to investigate Silver's character from yet another perspective (Figure 2–10).

Erin's sketch and her accompanying analysis amazed me. She had been intrigued by Long John Silver as a character, and Jennifer's sketch helped her to investigate this interest in new and unique ways. Once she had created the metaphor of the sea to represent Long John's mysterious character, she continued to build upon it by comparing species of fish to his personality traits.

Erin continued to draw connections from this experience over the next several months. As part of a culminating project for the novel study, she created a "three-dimensional visual" (her own terminology) to signify Long John's character. She found artifacts that symbolized his character traits, such as drama masks to signify his multifaceted personality and the way he covered up his true feelings, and she assembled them in a treasure box. Later, when the class studied the Holocaust, Erin continued to explore the idea of the inherent nature of people. She wondered if soldiers and civilians of either side could be simply labeled "good" or "bad." In some of the accounts we read, for example, Nazi soldiers showed compassion at the risk of their own lives. When I had the opportunity to talk with Erin's mother at the close of school, she remarked to me that Erin was still talking about people's appearances and their true natures. Erin had been interested in Long John Silver as a character, but it was Jennifer's sketch that fueled her continued inquiry for many months and in such a variety of contexts.

To me, reflecting upon creative decisions and thinking processes is the most crucial feature in an inquiring classroom. Unless the

Figure 2–10. Erin's visual

This visual represents Silver's heart. Clouds cover parts of it, because I don't think Silver ever completely reveals himself. There is a large cloud at the bottom because I don't think anybody knows what Silver is like at the bottom of his heart. I chose the sea to fill Long John Silver's heart because it is like him in many ways. It is mysterious, can be calm and quiet or rough and stormy, and is filled with many different personalities. The sea was also a big part of Silver's life. He was an experienced seaman. You might say "he had saltwater in his veins." On top of the water there is a ship, showing John's love of sailing. Part of the sea is calm and sunny, while the other half is rough and stormy. This shows how he could be nice or violent. As you go deeper into the ocean, you get to know Silver better. A shark represents how he could be bloodthirsty, wanting to kill the squire, captain, and doctor to get the treasure. His greed for treasure is symbolized by a tuna in a feeding frenzy. An angler fish shows how he lured Jim and everyone else to him by being polite and likable, when really he was scheming to get the treasure.

group had seen and discussed Jennifer's sketch, other students such as Erin would not have had the opportunity to extend those ideas. Examining authoring strategies collaboratively is crucial in using any communication system. We learn writing strategies by studying student and published authors. By enlarging our repertoire of expression using other means of communication such as art, we increase our avenues for inquiry and for exploration. We can then follow the same processes to author across multiple communication systems. Reflecting upon sketching strategies continues to open potential for making and sharing meaning.

A Student's View of Sketching and the Authoring Cycle

Seth's comment at the beginning of this chapter that authors' circles for sketches generate ideas "just like a writer" occurred in the context of a reflective time toward the end of his academic year. I had realized that talking with students, listening to their conversations with each other, and studying their work helped me understand the processes of authoring from fresh perspectives. I wanted to understand their views of our experiences from the entire year. I was curious to see what features of the authoring cycle were important to them, and how they expressed their understanding of the processes involved. Upon the advice of Carolyn Burke, I asked two classes to create sketches of "What happens when you sketch in response to reading." The students had a few days to think about their sketches and to create drafts. We then spent a class period meeting in groups of three or four in authors' circles to share our drafts and to collaborate about them. The students then had the opportunity to revise their sketches.

When we met in authors' circles, I tape-recorded several of the conversations to analyze how meaning developed through collaborative discussions. Seth's group helped me think more deeply about the parallels between writing and sketching and to appreciate the understanding that these young authors had developed about their processes of learning. Seth had created his sketch (Figure 2–11) in a rush.

Figure 2–11. Seth's visual

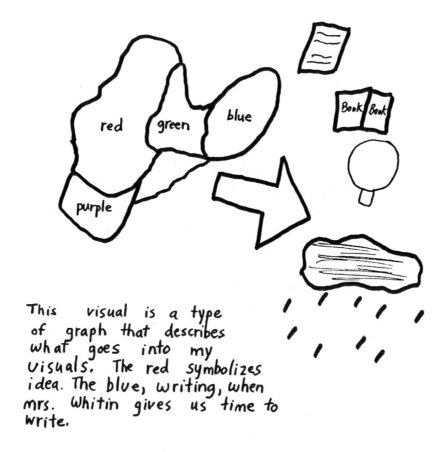

This visual is a type of graph that describes what goes into my visuals. The red symbolizes idea. The blue, writing, when mrs. Whitin gives us time to write.

Because the draft was unfinished, I could witness the evolution of his thought more easily. His thinking clearly changed as he conferred with his friends. He began by explaining his draft: "OK, right here I have a graph. It's just an odd shape I started out with my pencil and the paper, and it turned out an odd shape, a blob-kind of shape. The biggest part, the largest, where I get most of my ideas for my sketch-to-stretches, is just an idea. I have to think of an idea. That's what I usually do when I do a sketch-to-stretch, just start with a line. The blue is for when you (teacher) give us time to write, and I transfer my writing to a sketch. And then I understand. The purple is how I have to brainstorm, 'cause a lot of times I get stuck. It's like writer's block, but visual block. And I have this picture of the storm. I tried to make that shape in a brain, but I guess it didn't turn out. The green is when we do our groups, we all do one sketch-to-stretch. All our ideas build on it."

Brent, a member of Seth's authors' circle, commented that all the parts were "one big thing," and it went together. Seth continued to explain, "A sketch a lot of time comes from writing, 'cause you're reading writing, and sometimes you make a sketch-to-stretch off of your writing, so everything starts with writing." I knew from past experience that Seth usually sketched quickly and developed his ideas through discussion. At this point in the conversation, I became especially interested in the way that the group was supporting Seth connect reading, writing, and sketching in new ways.

As the group continued to talk, we realized that the group was generating new ideas through collaboration. Troy commented that developing ideas as a result of sharing with others was an important feature of sketching. He said, "When you look back on (a sketch), you see something you didn't see before. And when we're having group discussions, you can talk about it. Maybe somebody can answer your questions. And somebody will find some point, like the writing one (Seth's comment that "everything comes from writing"), and you think of some more ideas."

Seth jumped in next. "You could really go off from one sketch-to-stretch, then like in writing, revise it. And you'd have a new one from the ideas you've collected like we do in first period when we do those authors' circles. I would take a writing, and then we get ideas from that and write a new writing, and revise writing. And I think this (sketch) is kind of just a rough draft. And now that we're in here . . . I just thought of it. I related it to writing. And it is, 'cause here, it originates from writing. So when you're in an authors' circles (for visuals), you get ideas, and you revise it just like a writer."

Seth and his friends showed me what features of the authoring cycle were significant to them. Through art, language, and talk, these boys intuitively understood that authoring includes creating in any communication system (". . . you revise it just like a writer," "like writer's block, but visual block.") They acknowledged that receiving a text is active and generative (". . . and when we're having group discussions, and you think of some more ideas.") They valued the power of social interaction for both the author and the audience. They knew that knowledge or understanding is not stagnant but ever changing ("you get a new one from the ideas you've collected.") Reflecting upon the entire process of authoring enabled both the students and me to appreciate how all people make meaning.

THREE

Fostering a Spirit of Inquiry Through Sketching

Sometimes the craziest idea can get you the farthest.

DAVID, *Grade 7*

I thought a great deal about the lessons I learned through the *Summer of the Monkeys* study and through my reflections about the relationship between sketching and writing. I was especially impressed with (the importance of encouraging a spirit of playfulness while entertaining ideas.) By toying with multiple ideas, especially in conversation, the class would often deepen the entire group's understanding and appreciation of a story. I had changed a great deal as a teacher. A few years prior to this experience, I had taught the students the sketching strategy but had often assigned sketches as final projects to be completed at home. By encouraging students to create sketches in the midst of reading, we discovered a new potential. Initial sketches served as reference points as students continued to read and analyze the text. By providing them with the opportunity to sketch while in class, they were discovering the power of building upon one another's ideas. Over time, as I talked with students and studied their work, three features emerged as important in encouraging a spirit of inquiry in the study of literature. They are: (valuing mistakes, providing a wide variety of materials, and encouraging small group conversations.)

Valuing Mistakes: "We Made Something Work"

As I circulated around the room visiting literature circles one October day, Cynthia and Laura mentioned that they had been working on a collage for their book, *Roll of Thunder, Hear My Cry*, but they "couldn't think of what some of the colors meant." They had thrown their sketch away.

"What colors?" I asked.

"Yellow would be like Cassie because she is bright and had a lot of energy. We had brown because they were black people. Green stood for the land, but we couldn't think of the other colors."

I commented that I was sorry that they had thrown their collage away, because sometimes if people come back to their ideas later, they get new ideas. Cynthia dug into her book bag, muttering that maybe she still had it. She pulled out a piece of manila construction paper with colored ovals glued on it, overlapping. Brown marker squiggles surrounded the collage. She pointed to the yellow, green, and brown, explaining the significance again. "But we don't know what to do for the blue, orange, and violet."

The girls had created the collage first and then had tried to assign meaning to it. I had never seen this happen before and was intrigued. I suggested that they keep talking about the book and that ideas might come to them as they talked. In fact, by the end of class they thought that blue could be the rain in the story. I had another brief chat with them, and as we talked, I looked at the orange and realized that the orange could be associated with the major fire at the end of the book. I said, "I think I know one for orange. What about the end of the book?"

Cynthia replied, "Yeah, the fire."

This incident made me rethink my concept of sketching. Most of my experience with sketching followed a more linear progression: read, think, form images and symbols, and then draw. I had been comparing writing to sketching in my mind (the authoring cycle), but I had never encountered someone who made a visual and then assigned meaning to it. As I considered the significance of this event, I became more flexible about the process of creating. I wondered about the role of the sketch. It was clear that a sketch was far from an expression of one's thoughts. I wondered: Does a sketch change an author's thinking? What happens when a learner thinks, then sketches, then uses the sketch to think more about the reading? Is sketching a support for revisiting one's thoughts?

Shortly after this incident I began to watch for evidence that, with a concept of a story in mind, authors looked at their sketches for new meaning. Several instances helped me to investigate my hunches. For example, Brandi and Melanie were sketching the main character in the story "Bad Characters" by Jean Stafford (1984). Melanie offered to tell me about the sketch. Pointing to a very large eye in a profile view, she said, "Her eye is kind of sticking out because when she was caught shoplifting her eyes kind of went like this." Melanie demonstrated the effect by opening her eyes wide in mock surprise.

Brandi protested, "You just thought of that."

"I know," Melanie replied, "but it sounds good."

After the girls presented their project a few days later, Brandi wrote a reflection about what she learned by sketching her ideas for this story: "Melanie's mistake was a good one. We made something work that we thought didn't." The girls had sketched the main character, making the eye too large by mistake. When the girls explained their sketch to me, Melanie had thought back to the character's traits and the story events. Suddenly the large eye had new meaning for her; it could signify the shock and surprise the character had felt during the story. Her conclusion was logical, and both girls were satisfied with the additional meaning for their drawing. The sketch had helped these girls consider the story in a new way and make new connections among the events in the story. The sketch changed their thinking; it was not a final product.

That fall and winter I made a point of pushing the students to think about almost any line on their sketch, asking them to think back on the story to see if they could make any more connections. Group discussions were particularly exciting because we could generate a wide variety of possibilities. Later in the spring, though, I

Figure 3–1. Rachel's sketch "Gaston"

The girl is in the peach seed. She is kind of trapped inside, trying to decide who to be with. Her mother is reaching out to her. The dad has a small ♙ on his side and a ♥♡ because it shows that he is a nice person and she will be ☺ there. The ● has ※ in it to show that he can teach her alot of things. The mom has $ and a big ⌂ . She has a ☺ and is reaching out because she controls the girls life and the girl probably won't be happy.

——————

learned a new lesson about my own need to be a flexible thinker. I was talking with Rachel about her sketch, Figure 3–1, based on the story "Gaston" by William Saroyan (1984).

The story deals with the conflict between a young child and her divorced parents. In Rachel's sketch the girl is caught between her mother and her father. Rachel placed the little girl in the center of a peach because in the story the girl was fascinated with an imaginative tale that her father told to her about a bug in a peach. As Rachel was talking about her sketch, she suddenly noticed that the left hand of the father was missing. She pointed to the missing hand and said, "I didn't really mean to do that, not put a hand on. But now I'm kind of thinking about it, and it kind of goes, 'cause the mom was reaching out to her. And the dad didn't hold out his hand 'cause I guess you could say he didn't really have a say in it."

Rachel had not sketched a one-handed father intentionally. In talking with me she looked at her sketch more closely. She noticed that the hand was missing and created a hypothesis about its meaning. Over the course of the year the class had developed a belief that changing one's ideas was valuable. Earlier in the fall, Rachel had admitted to the class that they should have included the fairy ring on their poster when her group showed their project to the class (Figure 1–7). Now in the spring she was even more confident in her mental searching as she related her sketch to her understanding of the story. She used her sketch, mistake and all, to think more deeply about character relationships.

I was excited about Rachel's insights and shared them often with teachers. Later that spring I conducted a workshop about sketching and showed Rachel's sketch and story. When one teacher saw the visual she exclaimed, "It's a Venn diagram!"

I protested, "No, it's a peach!" As the words came out of my mouth, I realized what I had done. I had stopped being a flexible thinker. I had ignored the very nature of communication that I was using the sketch to demonstrate. The experience reminded me once again how much we learners depend upon others to grow. Others help to free us from our own narrowness. We can always think more broadly with the support of others than we can alone.

A Variety of Materials Encourages Broad Thinking

As my classes became more involved with the process of sketching, I began to appreciate artists' use of color, line, proportion, and symbol in new ways. I knew that my students would also make new connections to their reading and sketching through examining art, so I brought a collection of art slides to school. Looking at the slides, we discussed how the shapes and colors made us feel and what ideas or themes we connected to the paintings. For example, when we viewed Picasso's *Guernica*, we looked for the recurrent spike shapes and the distortion of human features. After a great deal of discussion, Karen remarked, "Maybe everything is distorted; when war happens, everything is crazy." Karen's idea summarized the connection between the lines and images in the painting and the feelings connected with the horrors of war.

On one occasion I was particularly impressed with the potential of using art slides to inspire sketching. One day we were looking at a slide of *Girl Crying*, also by Picasso. Half of the girl's face is red, while the other is yellow. The children were intrigued by this division of the face, and they began to make sense of it by connecting it to stories they had read. Michael thought that the painting could show the "good and bad sides" of the main character in "Bad Characters" (see Figure 4–3). Jill replied that the painting reminded her of a book that she was reading independently, in which a character resented her mother's remarriage, so she "loves her mother, but she hates her mother." The discussion of the painting helped the group tie together books of stories with similar themes or conflicts.

During this conversation I did not notice that Will had quietly taken some markers from his book bag and begun to sketch. After the discussion of the slide, the group spent the remaining part of the period reading, while I circulated around the room, responding to journal entries from the night before. When I stopped by Will's desk, I saw that he, too, had created a face divided into two colors, a Caucasian half and an African-American half (Figure 3–2).

I asked Will about his sketch. He explained that one side stood for Cassie in *Roll of Thunder, Hear My Cry* and the other represented Rose in *Rose Blanche*. He said that the two characters were alike because they both were exposed to discrimination. Cassie was confused about the way her race was treated, and Rose was concerned for the Jewish children in the concentration camp. Will told me that

Figure 3–2. Will's sketch

Comparison of Rose Blanche and Cassie Logan. This represents how Rose and Cassie's (Roll of Thunder) thoughts are related. They don't know they're supposed to treat others bad or be treated badly. They don't understand about the racism.

———

the similarity of the two characters had come to him when the class read *Rose Blanche* a few days before. Seeing Picasso's painting had provided an opportunity for Will to express his understanding of the thematic connections between two books that he read at entirely different points in the year. By committing his ideas to paper in this way, he was able to deepen his appreciation of both books, and share the connections he had made with the class. Will, the other members of the class, and I all benefited from studying artists from a sketcher's point of view.

The world of mathematical materials opened new potentials for thinking as well. While studying a collection of sketches with my husband David, we noticed that the representations and commentaries reflected several interesting mathematical concepts. For example, the chimpanzee's large proportion in Nathan and Troy's sketch (Figure 1–3) symbolized its importance in the story conflict. Many students devised ways to show time, such as the division of the *Summer of the Monkeys* project (Figure 1–7) into before and after sections. Students were also exploring graphing as a way to sketch. These mathematical concepts and strategies intrigued us, and I decided to purchase mathematical materials for the classroom. If the students were already using mathematical ideas to express their understanding of stories, I wanted to provide them with additional materials to pursue this interesting perspective. Among these materials were a set of circular, brightly colored plastic fraction pieces.

When the materials arrived I invited students to use them in whatever way they felt might help their visual exploration of representing ideas from stories. That day literature study groups were meeting to discuss *Treasure Island*. Stacey, Cara, and Laura called me over as they showed off an arrangement of the circular fraction pieces. Cara told me that she had created a pie graph of Jim Hawkins's character. She had used a green segment to show that Jim was "green with envy." Stacey showed her arrangement of a blue piece, a yellow piece, and a red piece. She explained, "Blue is for sadness because of his dad. Yellow because he's happy 'cause he killed Israel Hands. Red because he's angry at Long John Silver. Because he acted like a friend, but then he planned to kill them and stuff." I noticed that Stacey had used two red pieces, and there was a single yellow and a single blue. I asked her why she had used two reds, and only one of each of the other colors. Stacey pointed to the red section, which was composed of two pieces, and continued, "It's really to fill up the circle, but he's really mad, so we used two reds."

I pressed Stacey further. "So two reds even though it's the same amount of space as yellow, two pieces means sort of . . ." "Really mad."

Even though the two red pieces covered the same amount of space as the single yellow, the girls used the idea that the number of pieces could show the intensity of Jim's anger. *Two* means "twice as much" figuratively. The fraction materials gave the girls an opportunity to play with their ideas in a new way. In a sketch they probably would have drawn single red, yellow, and blue sections. In order to fill the circle with plastic pieces, they had needed to use two reds to make the equivalent fraction shown by the yellow. The idea of *two* helped them extend their understanding of the character relationships in a new way. The new materials had opened a new potential for thinking.

Next, the girls began to rearrange the pieces and to create new interpretations. Suddenly Laura announced, "I have an oxymoron." I was intrigued with her statement. I had encouraged the class to play with the idea of character oxymorons for the book. We had talked about which of the characters could have been labeled "dangerously friendly." We had described events in the plot as "exciting terror" or as "lucky mistakes." Never in our conversations, however, had we connected the idea of an oxymoron to a sketch. I sensed that something exciting was about to happen with this conversation. Laura explained, "Fearfully friendly. Friendly would have to be a bright color, sort of like yellow would be, so I used yellow in half the circle for friendliness. And then fear would be red, sort of a scary color, and when people get angry, they get red in the face. So angry people are scared, so red." I was amazed at Laura's thinking. I realized that the bright colors of the pieces and their obvious division into distinct halves had helped her connect the idea of opposites in language to opposites involving physical materials.

Cara jumped in with her idea. Pointing to a half-red, half-yellow arrangement, she exclaimed, "That's my oxymoron. One time I wrote in my journal 'bitterly sweet.'" Now Cara was mentally scanning the verbal oxymorons that she had created, and she was translating those ideas into the colors and sizes of the pieces.

Then I joined the fun. The idea of needing two reds to create the equivalent size of one yellow piece had encouraged me to wonder about the nature of oxymorons themselves. Oxymorons by definition are pairs of opposites, yet the fraction pieces invited us to divide a circle into various fractions. I wondered aloud, "Do oxymorons always have to be half-and-half, do you think?"

Figure 3–3a and 3–3b. Pie graph oxymorons

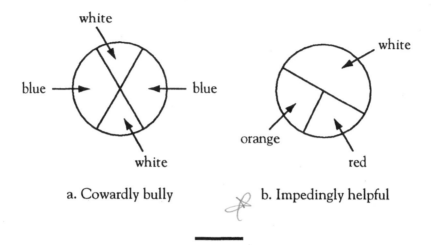

a. Cowardly bully   b. Impedingly helpful

Laura answered, "Probably you could do a different type of oxymoron with three ideas."

"Oooo," I exclaimed. "I've never tried one three ways. Three ways . . . a triangular oxymoron." I was toying with the idea that we might be able to develop a three-way oxymoron with shades of meaning for three words.

As I thought, Cara commented, "You could do them different ways, too." The girls continued to move the pieces around, no longer arranging them into distinct halves.

Stacey created the next idea, a split shape of two blue thirds placed over a single white whole (Figure 3–3a). "Cowardly, white for purity and everything. And blue for bully. That seems like a mean color. I guess it would be like this. I don't know who they're talking about (which character), but the bully takes up more, and the white is less."

Laura contributed one more oxymoron, composed of an orange with a red placed on top of it on one side, both covering part of the white whole, which was left exposed on other side (Figure 3–3b). "All right, impedingly helpful. Impeding means getting in the way, so I thought, orange and red, 'cause they clash. And the white stands for purity, so it's like a helpful color—a good deed is color."

Laura and Stacey had built upon my idea that oxymorons could be composed of more than two distinct elements. Stacey's "cowardly bully" showed that the oxymoron was composed of "weighted" opposites. The pieces showed that the idea of "bully" was more important than the idea of "cowardly." Laura used clashing colors, red and orange, to intensify her idea that "getting in the way" diminished "help."

This conversation and these new ways of thinking never would have occurred without the plastic fraction pieces. Since we could move the pieces around quickly, we could shift their positions quickly and create new arrangements. In other words, the girls could "revise" their "texts" easily. We did not have to cross out, place arrows on our paper, start over, or revise in any of the ways we did with paper and pencil. We simply could move the pieces and express a new thought. The pieces invited a spirit of playfulness, and it is often in playfulness that we develop unique ideas.

This experience showed me ties between art, mathematics, and language. We explored elements of art (symbolic colors), mathematics (size, proportion, number), and language (oxymorons), combining them in new ways through a spirit of inquiry. For example, the sharply divided halves of color supported Laura to think of oxymorons. Looking at the fractional pieces with *oxymorons* as a frame of reference helped all of us to generate multiple new ideas. Cara reviewed oxymorons that she had created mentally and created new ways to show her ideas. The girls and I developed new layers of meaning for oxymorons by playing with the idea that oxymorons did not need to be composed of equally weighted pairs.

I learned a lot about myself and my role as a teacher through this experience as well. I was an active learner in the group. The girls helped me to think in new ways, and my tentative wondering encouraged them to extend their thinking in turn. Connecting their use of two red pieces to show an intense feeling with the idea of an oxymoron, I thought of a new possible definition of this concept. I was genuinely eager to try out the idea with the pieces, and I was excited as the girls pursued my idea. In this event all four of us were enriching our individual thinking and creating deeper ideas collaboratively. I never could have anticipated the events of that day, and it influenced my changing understanding of teaching and learning. I was realizing more and more that my active role as a learner was a more powerful demonstration than any lesson could ever be.

Encouraging Informal Conversations

The experience with Laura, Cara, and Stacey showed me the importance of providing time to talk informally and to play with ideas. I realized that through our collaborative exploration, I myself had changed as a learner. Certainly my students deserved the same ongoing opportunity, but, like other teachers, I worried about using time effectively in class. I needed to know more about the value of informal conversation in literature circles. Cara soon taught me another important lesson about this power of collaboration.

One day shortly before our fraction-piece exploration Cara and her literature circle were discussing reader's responses that they had created the night before for homework. When I came by to chat with the girls during class, I saw Laura's sketch (Figure 3–4).

Laura said that she was showing that Jim was scared but excited and that the bad guys outnumbered the good guys. She said that the exclamation marks showed that he was scared and excited at the same time. I wanted to encourage her to extend her thinking, so I asked if the box could mean anything. At first she said "No, it was just a box." Stacey, listening to the conversation, remarked that during this part of the story maybe Jim was "in a box." Laura thought for a few seconds and said that maybe Jim was "trapped . . . because he's without his friends." The box, which at first had not been a meaningful element for Laura, was becoming more symbolic through our conversation.

Next Stacey volunteered to show her sketch since, she, too, had drawn a box (Figure 3–5).

As we looked at her sketch, Stacey explained that Jim was caught between being a man and being a boy. She realized that

Figure 3–4. Laura's sketch

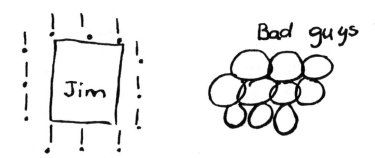

This shows the way Jim feels when he is with all the bad guys. He's scared but still excited. It also shows how Jim was outnumbered by the bad guys.

———

Figure 3–5. Stacey's sketch

This is to show that in the beginning Jim was caught between boyhood and manhood. He wanted to grow up, but he's really scared about what will happen to him if he was a man. Therefore, he is closer to boyhood than to manhood.

———

being caught between boyhood and manhood was a "big idea" in the book. Cara, who had been quiet until this time, looked again at Stacey's drawing and remarked that maybe Jim was feeling tight and closed in. We then returned to Stacey's comment of a "big idea" and began a conversation about other books that we had read over the course of the year that showed a similar theme of maturity. Cara contributed ideas to this part of our discussion as well. Although Cara had not sketched that day, she was active in constructing meaning in the group. The influence of this conversation became more apparent later. For the time being, however, we had collaboratively used the concept of a box to explore figurative meanings ("trapped," "caught," "closed in") and to explore the ideas of internal conflict and character maturation as an intertextual theme.

Within ten days both Stacey and Cara shared sketches that branched from the ideas generated from the "box" conversation with their group. On the day of the "pie graph oxymorons" the girls used the plastic pie graph pieces to show Jim's anger to Israel Hands and his happiness after the murder. As they talked, Cara recalled their earlier conversation about the box. As Cara studied one of the arrangements of fraction pieces, she remarked, "He's equally amount of happy. He has mixed-up feelings. Like the mixed-up feelings between adulthood and childhood." Cara's comment reminded Stacey to tell me that she had sketched a "sequel" to her box sketch, and she reached for her journal. She pointed to her sketch (Figure 3–6).

Stacey had pursued her "big idea" of Jim's maturation. She had used her previous sketch and the group's conversation as a reference point. I was also interested that Stacey chose to use exclamation

Figure 3–6. Stacey's sequel

boyhood manhood

After Jim killed Israel Hands, he felt a lot more like a man, but he still isn't quite there.

---

points in this sketch, as Laura had done earlier. The collaborative discussion and Laura's visual had helped Stacey as she compared Jim's behavior at two different points in the novel.

It was later that I discovered how the conversations had affected Cara. Reviewing her portfolio a few weeks later, I found the sketch shown in Figure 3–7.

I had not seen this sketch in Cara's journal, which had been made two days after our exploration with the fraction pieces. Her

Figure 3–7. Cara's sketch

I have made a sketch-to-stretch. The 1st box means when Jim was realy exited about getting the treasure, and the 2nd box was when they found out the treasure was gone. The boxes kind of represent Jim's heart.

Portfolio commentary: I chose this reader's response because it shows my growth as a thinker. I thought long and hard, trying to come up with a sketch-to-stretch and I thought about this. Before I had trouble thinking of sketch-to-stretches, but this was the first time I thought long and hard about it.

portfolio commentary impressed me, particularly when she said, "Before I had trouble trying to come up with a sketch." Apparently she felt much more confident now. I decided to talk to her about her sketch and her feelings as an author.

Cara first admitted to me that when she did most of her reader's responses, "I don't really think about it that hard." She felt in particular that her sketches were "kind of weak." She explained that this sketch was strong, however, because she had spent fifteen minutes looking through the book seeing at what points Jim was happy and sad. She realized that Jim was "more happy than he was sad, and that's why this box is smaller" (pointing to the cube on the right). Then she had "thought of other classes like math. And we had learned how to draw these, so I just decided, hey! that's a good idea 'cause I can show the inside of it. When people think, they don't always show what they're thinking on the outside. And then the inside is what they really think." She had thought of Jim Hawkins during the events of the story. "I had to figure out some of the happy thoughts. I could tell he was a little bit sad, too. When he was happy, he was covering up. One time with Long John Silver, he was talking to him, and he had just found out about the apple barrel. Long John Silver came up to him and he acted like he was happy, but he was *really* thinking something else."

The conversations about the box idea and our playful exploration with the fraction pieces had helped Cara explore sketching more deeply. I was impressed with the way that she connected the idea of a box with the potential of a drawing of a cube that she had learned in math. She extended the idea of a two-dimensional figure to a three-dimensional one, and she justified her sketch with specific details from the book. I wondered if Cara herself felt that her literature circle had encouraged her growth and asked her if anybody else's sketch or any discussion besides math class helped her. She answered, "At first I didn't draw that many sketch-to-stretches, but then when Stacey did that one about Jim being between childhood and manhood, I thought I should start doing that 'cause those are really interesting."

Now I was really interested, asking, "If you had to say what was important to the class to encourage or explore sketches, what would you say some of those factors would be?"

Cara answered thoughtfully. "First of all what could really help you is just looking through the book. And looking at other people's sketch-to-stretches would help you. An inspiration, I guess. Just looking, just get inspired by them, and you could probably do it 'cause that's how I did it. Not all people are like me but, like, I mainly got inspired by others."

I thought a great deal about our conversation in the days and months that followed. Without her group, Cara probably would not have created her cube sketch. She developed an interest in exploring ideas through sketching by playing with possible meanings for Stacey's and Laura's boxes, and she began to take new risks in sketching on her own. She did not copy the work of her friends; she built upon their ideas by combining them with her own. She drew from her larger world of experience, such as math class, for potential ideas to connect with her reading. Her active pursuit for ideas strengthened her commitment to analysis of her reading. As she saw more value in her response journal, she studied the book "long and hard." When she selected the sketch to include in her portfolio, she realized how much she had grown as a reader and a thinker. She was much more confident. With the support of others, Cara had changed.

However, I also suspected that more people were like Cara than she realized. We all get "inspired by others." She, too, had contributed to the learning of others. The members of her literature group benefited from Cara's ideas about the connections between the box conversations and the ideas generated by the fraction pieces. My thinking, too, had been enriched by the conversations with all of the members of the literature circle. Every one of us was "inspired."

Fostering a Spirit of Inquiry

Toward the end of the year Malti wrote, "When you create a sketch-to-stretch, you need to think about everything. Color, size, shape, and texture are a few ideas. Everyone has a different way to make their picture. Usually a visual has hidden messages that make it more interesting." When I thought about Malti's comment, I realized that through it she expressed the features of a spirit of inquiry that we had developed as a class. First, in her comment Malti acknowledges that "everything" contributes to the potential meaning of a sketch: color, size, shape, and texture. Having a wide variety of materials to explore can help learners discover new perspectives for expressing ideas. Secondly, Malti realizes that each person has unique ideas. When "Everyone has a different way to make their picture," and everyone shares with each other, the group benefits from their collective understanding. (Both teacher and students grow through "everyone's ideas" by reading and viewing each other's work, and by talking about our thinking.) Studying the published work of artists broadens our understanding of "everyone's ideas" as well. Finally, Malti illustrates the heart of inquiry in her comment. Inquiry never holds final answers; it is an ongoing, intriguing adventure. Malti wants to be challenged by "hidden messages." By valuing "mistakes" and by exploring possible meanings collaboratively, we open new potentials. The more we look, the more we wonder, and the more we grow.

FOUR

Specialized Sketching:
The Story of Literature Pie Graphs

When I do a sketch-to-stretch, I think drawing. It gets out my feelings more. I draw something down. They say a picture's worth a thousand words. So I think that drawing represents more than writing. You get more out of it just by looking at it and drawing it. Kind of like a graph.

TROY, *Grade 7*

As a graduate of my seventh-grade class, Derek returned to visit on the first day of school the following August. He strode into the room, scanned the walls, and jested me. "What, no pie graphs?" His remark helped me to see that graphing as a visual response to literature had become part of the identity of our class. I reflected back to the beginning of the previous school year. I never would have anticipated that this group of students would invent and develop a complex symbol system that I had never seen before. Derek and his classmates taught me to value deeply the power of collaboration over time in an inquiring classroom.

The Invention of a Tool

Making pie graphs to show ideas in literature began early in the year. One day in September Samantha sketched while the members of

Figure 4–1a and 4–1b. Samantha's visual and revised draft for *All Together Now*

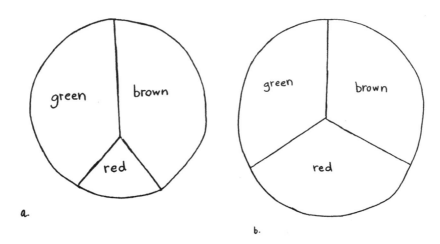

a.

b.

This is to symbolize that Casey wanted peace for severel reasons. One reason is she wanted peace in the world so her dad could come back. Another reason is she wanted peace for Dwayne because she doesn't want him to go to the hospital. She wants peace between Hazard and Pansy and Taylor and Gwen. Casey is not the only one who wants peace.

her literature study group, Seth and Malti, discussed the novel *All Together Now*. After a few minutes she announced, "This is powerful!" and showed her group a peace symbol made of green, brown, and red (Figure 4–1a). She explained that the different parts symbolized the main character's—Casey—desire for peace in the Korean War, for peace between her friend Dwayne and his brother, and for peaceful solutions to two rocky romantic relationships between other characters. The red section, which symbolized love, was smaller. Seth asked Samantha why that part was smaller. She sighed that she had "messed up." Seth's question helped Samantha to reflect upon the ideas in the book, and when she revised her draft (Figure 4–1b), she was careful to make all three sections equal.

Although I never heard the students mention the word graph, the balanced proportion and the circular shape of her representation gave the final product the appearance of a pie graph. Her revised sketch became part of her group's culminating novel project. She shared Figure 4–1b with the class, and it was posted on the wall for several weeks.

Within a month Troy created a more traditional pie graph (Figure 4–2) to show characters' feelings in the beginning of *Roll of Thunder, Hear My Cry*. He chose to label and divide the characters' feelings into different parts, and he decided to indicate the importance of each by varying the proportion of areas shown. Troy's pie graph became important to the entire class later in the year.

The percentages highlighted the mathematical dimension of his sketch. Although I did not ask Troy to share his graph with the large group when he sketched it originally, he did show it to his literature study group. Several months later, I photocopied Troy's graph along with several others, so that the class could discuss graphing as a response to reading.

Another event that contributed to the pie graph theme occurred about a month after Troy sketched his graph of feelings. Nathan, Brent, and Jeremy, along with the class, had read "Bad Characters." In the story Emily, the main character, befriends a charismatic figure, Lottie, who leads her to shoplift. After a discussion they decided that Emily felt half good and half bad about Lottie. They created their graph (Figure 4–3) to show Emily's attitude toward Lottie.

When they presented their completed visual to the group, the precision of the graph was the catalyst for a lively conversation. The discussion contrasted with the class sharing described in Chapter 1 (Figure 1–7), in which the group explored alternative meanings together. The first students to comment remarked about the format of the sketch. Melanie commented that she liked the way the boys had put the sad colors on one side and the happy colors on the opposite side. Lisa followed with a comment that she liked it because it looked like a graph. Samantha, taking a cue from Lisa, added, "It's

Figure 4–2. Troy's sketch

My graph shows how the Logan family probably felt.

———

like a pie graph. Precise measures of how they felt." Samantha's comment implied that graphs, or even mathematical ideas in general, are "precise measures."

During the next part of the conversation, the class found that the contrary was true; this graph could *not* convey "precise measures." The next students who talked began to challenge the boys' interpretation that divided Emily's view of Lottie into half-good, half-bad. Seth was particularly vehement about his disagreement. He

Figure 4–3. Collaborative graph of "Bad Characters"

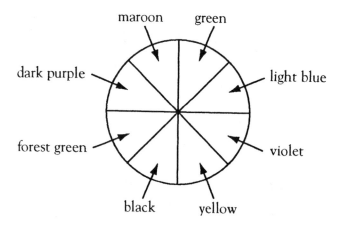

This drawing is to represent how Emily thought or felt about Lottie, a good side and a bad side. We chose happy colors for the good side, and we chose dark and sad colors for the bad side. Emily felt like she wanted to be around Lottie part of the time, and another part of the time she did not want to be around her. She liked Lottie because she did things so smoothly and without thought, like it was all planned out ahead of time. She also liked Lottie because Lottie liked her. But, the reason she didn't like Lottie was because she stole. When she first met Lottie, she liked her because she was different from all her old friends. But when she found out that she stole, it was kind of a shock to her. It was like the best thing that ever happened to her had blown up in her face. But she stuck with it, went through with the stealing, and she got in trouble. She also lost yet another friend.

———

objected, "She (Emily) did like her a lot. I think she regrets . . . she felt bad that she had stolen. But that was the only bad part."

Nathan responded in defense. He felt that taken as a whole, the half-half notion was accurate. "Listen, before she like found out she stole and everything, it was all good colors, but when she found out she stole and stuff, it halved it out."

Seth was not satisfied. He replied that the reason Emily almost stole was that she liked Lottie so much. The half-bad description was inaccurate. "No, she went along with it 'cause she really liked Lottie." Emily's pinch of conscience was the only bad part of her relationship with Lottie. Seth explained, "That's (conscience) the only bad side, so I think that shouldn't take up half of her! If it was strong enough to be half of it, then she wouldn't have done it [stolen]."

The class discussion was showing me that the "truth" implied by a precise-looking graph could be questioned by skeptics. Seth was giving evidence from the text (that Emily had gone to the store with the intention of shoplifting) to prove his interpretation that the "good" side should be larger. Nathan, on the other hand, saw a change in Emily's feelings. At first Emily practically worshiped Lottie, but when she found out that she was both a thief and a liar, her feelings were "halved out." I had a hunch that Seth was looking at the importance of individual events, while Nathan was taking a more global stance. I wanted the authors to explain the thinking behind their sketch in more depth so the class could explore this difference in interpretation. I asked the boys if the graph represented the story as a whole, and the discussion that ensued led the class to discover a limitation of pie graphs.

Nathan confirmed my belief that the graph did show the story as a whole. I followed by asking if the graph might have looked different if they had sketched at the beginning or the end of the story. Nathan replied, "It's an average proportion. But like at the very beginning, she was kind of uneasy about her because she knew she was trying to steal stuff. But then when she talked to her and she said, 'Let's go through your mother's bureau,' she figured out she was kind of like her 'cause she always went through her mother's bureau. So it was kind of whole then, or almost whole. And then she found out that she steals all the time, then it kind of went a little bit less. Then she found out she does it [steals] all the time; she does it for fun, and it kind of went back to even."

Brent joined Nathan saying that they had to take an average of the story, and as he began to explain with "because we couldn't do . . . ," Nathan interrupted to complete the idea, "Like thirty different times."

Brent continued, "At different parts of the story there's like a rapid change."

The discussion revealed that graphs may be useful to show over-all proportion, but they do not convey individual events at different points in time. At the beginning of the story Emily thought Lottie was terrific, but at the end of the story Emily was disappointed in her. The graph could not capture those variations of feelings. This limitation challenged members of the class to invent new tools of expression in their graphs. Some of these tools included different uses of line, such as broken or jagged, word labels, and thoughtful placement of the segments.

Exploring New Ways to Graph

Seth created a "heart pie graph," (Figure 4–4) just days after the "Bad Characters" discussion. This graph described the feelings of characters in *The Road to Memphis* (Taylor 1990).

Seth's sketch capitalized on the potential of graphs to show general proportions of feelings as Troy had done (Figure 4-2). He also added jagged lines to signify tension and conflict, as well as character names to clarify his meaning. His and other students' experimentation showed that they were making strategic decisions about the use of pie graphs based on our class discussions.

One such sketch was Sarah's. Sarah created a colorful pie graph in response to the novel *Where the Lilies Bloom* in December. Her colors, like Samantha's (Figure 4–1a and 4–1b), symbolized feelings or events in the book, but she added a quote from the book next to each section to justify her choices. For example, next to the red section that represented love, Sarah quoted a sentence that described the enamored look in a couple's eyes. Sarah's use of quotes showed that she anticipated defending her graph to her study group. Despite this added dimension for the sake of clarity, one of the groups that responded to Sarah's graph disputed the size of her largest section. As I read the second group's written comments to Sarah, it seemed to me that sketches with a mathematical dimension elicited a differ-ent kind of response than more pictorial or symbolic ones. Graphs

Figure 4–4. Seth's heart graph

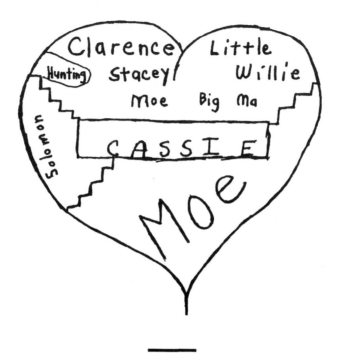

seemed to send a message of authority and precision to audiences, and discussions reflected this implied value. My observations led me to become even more interested in this mathematical dimension of sketching. I began to scrutinize student journals and portfolios for patterns among the responses.

In January I found a pie graph and commentary in Heidi's portfolio that intrigued me. As I examined Heidi's sketch (Figure 4–5), I decided to talk with her about her graph. I needed to understand more about the students' perceptions of this graphing offshoot of sketching. Heidi's interview spurred a class investigation greater than any I had ever experienced. As Derek's comment at the beginning of the chapter showed, we had become "the pie graph class."

Figure 4–5. Heidi's graph of *Fallen Angels* and portfolio comment

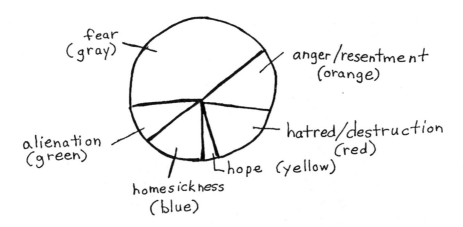

The mind of a Nam soldier (esp. Perry)

These feelings going through the mind of a soldier are supposed to be proportionate (the biggest sections, the ones they feel the most of) disregard length, though, and just look at width.

Fear is the gray, brooding feeling felt keenest—sometimes prominent, sometimes subdued, always there.

Homesickness, the second largest, the soldiers are blue, they miss home and can't wait to get back to "the world."

Anger/resentment and red hatred/destruction are third in size, and closely related in color. The soldiers are angry about being in Nam, the food, the disease, and discomfort, they resent the draft. They hate (most of them) the Cong, and wish to destroy all the Communists.

Alienation, tying in with Fear and homesickness and is similar.

Portfolio comment: I was looking out for a chance to use the pie graph idea, and here it came! I was able to depict the feelings of the characters in the book. In doing this sketch-to-stretch, I was forced to look at the people in the book more closely, to imagine what they'd be feeling. It was an exercise in putting myself in their place.

Heidi had sketched a pie graph to explore the feelings of the main character, Perry, in *Fallen Angels* (Myers 1988). She chose to include this graph as one of her most significant reader's responses from the second nine-week grading period.

When I asked Heidi about her portfolio comment, "I was looking for a chance to use the pie graph idea, and here it came!" Heidi explained:

> It seemed like a lot of people were doing that (making pie graphs). And then I decided that would be a good way to show the different relationships and the different things that happened and the different degrees that they were in. And I thought what can I do that was really relevant to the story. And then I realized that a lot of what the story's about is the way they feel about Vietnam, so I thought I'd draw a pie graph that shows the different things that they were feeling when they were in Vietnam. How they'd be there without wanting to be there. And I thought of all the different things that it could be, and the colors I could use, and which one they felt the most, which one they felt the least, and all the different things in between. And then, what the different colors meant. So what are the different sizes (so that the size of the section would correlate with the importance of the feeling).

As Heidi observed her classmates inventing pie graphs, and as she studied them in displays in the room, she had begun to sort out in her mind what a pie graph could or could not do to signify ideas in a story. She had decided that pie graphs were most helpful in showing relationships of feelings and "the different degrees that they were in." She had wanted to do a pie graph, but in her mind, she needed the type of story that would be enhanced through this kind of analysis. Heidi based her generalization on the evolving social knowledge of the class, yet when she sketched her visual, she created her own personal invention as well. Although other students had used color to represent feelings in visuals, Heidi used shades of related colors to convey closely associated feelings. I asked Heidi about these colors and their relationships as we talked.

Heidi explained that her color choice came from her study of warm and cool colors in art class. She had intentionally used red and orange because they were "related." Although she had not originally thought that blue was related to green and gray, she later realized that they, too, "were similar"; they all were cool colors. She had begun her sketch by trying to make the colors represent feelings and ideas. "You know, if you're depressed or down, you say you're blue. And the green, there's green forests in Vietnam, and gray—fear is kind of gray, dark and foreboding, but it's not dark and black. Orange is the closest thing I could get to red, so I used red again. And yellow is like light and lighter—like that candle Vanessa did, but her candle was peace." [Vanessa was another student who had used yellow in response to another novel about Vietnam.]

I saw that Heidi had used colors in a slightly different way from her classmates. Although she used colors to represent feelings, she had connected the idea of warm and cool colors to emotions. This tie led her to choose two related warm colors, red and orange, to convey the similar feelings of anger and hatred. She also used similar size segments of the graph to show further the balance between these two emotions. Her commentary had not reflected an intentional decision to put these two sections next to each other, however, so I had written a comment to her in her journal about the possibility of location as a symbol, too, mentioning that the placement of the two related sections next to each other seemed to highlight their similarity. As we talked I asked her to respond to my comment. She replied that she had put them next to each other because they were related feelings, but she had not meant to emphasize their similarity by placing them in this way. The placement was more a reflection of the order in which she thought of the feelings.

By now I had raised a lot of questions about pie graphs in my mind. I had questioned whether Heidi had intentionally chosen to put two similar feelings next to each other, thereby highlighting their similarity in color and size. My raising the question opened up the possibility that the similarity in size and color, in conjunction with proximity, could serve to convey ideas. Along with the class,

I was exploring the potential of the knowledge that we were creating as a group. I could not separate my inquiry from the inquiry of the group. We were supporting one another as we made meaning together.

Delving Deeper into Graphs

As I became more and more engrossed in my desire to investigate the potential of these literature pie graphs, I began to conduct more small group and whole class meetings to ask the students their perceptions of the graphing experiences. These meetings radically changed my understanding of the power of teacher research. Although my initial intent for the meetings was to have the students help me understand the nature of our explorations with graphing, I did not realize the power of my own demonstration of inquiry. My genuine interest in graphing raised the students' awareness of its potential because we made our authoring decisions, our wonderings, and our anomalies public through discussion. It was my intensity as a teacher-researcher in wanting to know more about their sketches that further developed the shared knowledge of the group. These exploratory discussions supported the invention of new symbols as we collaboratively tried to solve problems of conveying our ideas clearly. As individual learners shared with the entire group, we all had more demonstrations upon which to draw for future sketches.

We spent an entire class period looking at examples of the variety of pie graphs that had been created. I asked the students what they thought could be successfully conveyed with pie graphs, and what was left ambiguous through this medium. Members of the group felt that it was difficult to show details in graphs. For example, Nathan and his group had shown Emily's feelings to be "half good and half bad" (Figure 4–3). At different points in the story, however, the character had felt either all good or all bad. The graph illustrated an "average" of feelings. Individual incidents could be lost through graphing. Most of the class believed, on the other hand, that graphs were useful to show general feelings and relationships between feelings. Graphs also served to generate conversations in groups because authors were forced to justify the proportions that they had chosen.

By the end of class our discussion had raised some interesting issues. Wanting to know more, I invited a small group of students to review the transcript of this discussion and to continue exploring these ideas. A group of eight volunteered to help me.

When we assembled before school one morning, Jill was eager to show her friends a graph she had constructed on the previous day. Apparently the whole class discussion, as well as the recent addition of the geometric materials to the classroom, had piqued her interest. She pulled from her book bag a sketch (Figure 4–6) that she called an "octagonagraph."

Jill had divided the octagon into eight triangles. Each triangle represented a character from *Treasure Island*. Some of the triangles were shaded with two or more colors. The colors symbolized character traits, and triangles with several colors signified multiple traits. Jill's graph showed some unique features of a graph. First, its shape was different from any of the graphs sketched previously. Secondly, it was the only graph thus far created in which a section was composed of more than one color. These new features interested Jill's audience. The group talked with Jill about her sketch, and they also questioned her about her decisions. They asked such questions as, "How come Dr. Livesey is part bad?" "How do you know the parrot is bad?" Jill's choice of symbols and the group's questions concerning her authoring decisions influenced the thinking of several students, as I was to discover within a few days.

Before school the next morning Doug showed me a new graph that was clearly influenced by Jill's octagonagraph (Figure 4–7). When he told me with no prompting that Jill's octagonagraph had influenced him, I decided to talk with him more. He explained what he had been thinking after our morning discussion. "I thought of Jill's and I thought I could make something like it, and I thought it was a neat idea. I thought I could make something look like that 'cause I thought that was a neat idea using the colors and the pie graph to explain about the characters. I didn't want to copy it, so I sat down and thought about it for awhile, and I just went from there." Pointing to Jill's graph he said, "See how Captain Smollett's divided up into brown and red and orange? I thought about how

Figure 4–6. Jill's "octagonagraph" of *Treasure Island*

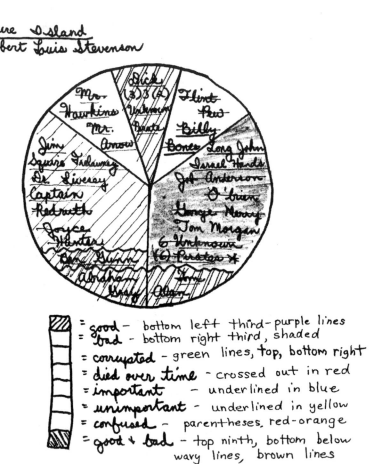

= good — bottom left third – purple lines
= bad — bottom right third, shaded
= corrupted — green lines, top, bottom right
= died over time — crossed out in red
= important — underlined in blue
= unimportant — underlined in yellow
= confused — parentheses, red-orange
= good & bad — top ninth, bottom below
wavy lines, brown lines

Flint, Pew, Billy Bones — not on boat,
bad side
Mr. Hawkins, Mr. Arrow — not on boat,
good side

Figure 4–7. Doug's graph

characters
ON BOAt

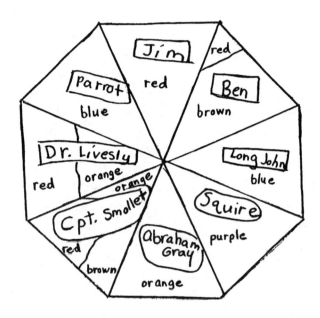

Blue = bad
Brown = unknown
orange = almost all good
red = good
purple = half and half
green = almost all bad Little good

you could divide things up into a lot of different categories. They don't have to be just one." Jill's use of multicolored segments had supported Doug to extend her idea through his own personal invention.

After Doug and I had talked, I reviewed the transcript of the small-group morning discussion. I found that during the meeting Doug had said that one reason pie graphs are helpful is that "Everybody knows what a pie graph is." That comment acknowledged the fact that pie graphs are part of the group's social or cultural knowledge, or codes. Pie graphs were a format that conveyed shared meanings to the entire class. Jill had personalized that code by creating her octago-nagraph in which characters were represented by different colors, and in which characters were shown to have multiple traits. Her sketch challenged the statement made by several students during our whole class discussion, that pie graphs "could not show detail." When Jill shared her sketch with the group, her personal invention or code of showing detail became public. Doug built upon her invention by using the idea that more than one character trait could be represented simultaneously. In turn Doug created a new set of personal codes as he symbolized both story events and character traits. Doug and Jill demonstrated that our classroom community shared social codes and knowledge, but that each class member continued to express personal inventiveness while borrowing from those codes.

A few days later I found that another member of our morning discussion group, Malti, had borrowed from Jill's demonstration in a different way. Malti had created Figure 4–8 on the evening of our collaborative meeting, the same night that Doug had sketched his character graph.

I remembered that during the meeting Malti, who had not yet sketched any pie graphs, had mentioned that maybe she "would try pie graphs now." Our discussion had served as an invitation for her to explore this form of sketching. However, Malti extended Jill's idea in her own way. She told me, "We were talking about like is there some reason to put things next to each other, 'cause we were talking about Jill's where her little orange went over into her blue." Whereas Doug was interested in how more than one color in the same section of a

Figure 4–8. Malti's graph

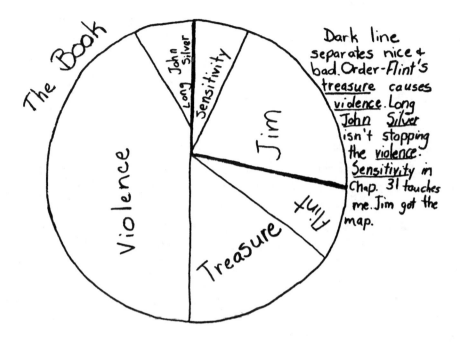

Dark line separates nice and bad. Order—Flint's treasure causes violence. Long John Silver isn't stopping the violence. Sensitivity in Chap. 31 touches me. Jim got the map.

graph could be used to show multiple traits of a character, Malti was interested in the juxtaposition of sections that could highlight the relationship between two characters. These two students' comments helped me to understand that a single demonstration, in this case Jill's octagonagraph, could be interpreted by learners in different ways to serve new purposes. Since the learners themselves made their own strategic decisions of what to borrow, they felt empowered as authors of new ideas. When I reflected upon these various graphs, I realized that the power and value of demonstrations in a supportive learning community lies in their open-ended nature.

Malti's interest in the placement of sections pushed me to review once again the transcript of our before-school discussion. I wanted to look closely at our comments about this feature. What had happened that had spurred Malti's interest? I found that I had asked Jill if she had put characters next to each other intentionally, and she had replied, "No." I realized that in this case intentionality was denied, but raising the *possibility* of intentionality had been a powerful invitation for Malti. She had begun to ask herself, "*What if* the placement of the characters on the graph *did* matter?" We were developing a spirit of "what if"—a playful, exploratory sense in the classroom —and Malti capitalized on that inquisitive stance by exploring this particular alternative through her own personal invention.

In fact, the issue of placement did become even more important to Malti in the days that followed. Two weeks later she created a pie graph to show the events of a mystery, *And Then There Were None* (Christie 1977). As Malti wrote her commentary, she said aloud emphatically to a small group that was watching her "No order. No particular color" (Figure 4–9).

Malti realized that her audience might ask her about her intentions. Even though she did not place the elements near one another purposely, she realized that placement was a consideration that needed to be addressed. Malti knew the shared norms of the class well. Her statement shows that authors' anticipating a response from an audience is part of social knowledge. Authors of language, art, or any communication system carry around in their heads a sense of audience. This concept of audience influences the decisions they make and the intentions they wish to convey. Malti's actions showed that authors are never alone when they compose.

I was with the group of students who were watching Malti sketch this second pie graph. When she said that there was no particular color or order, I asked, "But why did you choose to make your graph in a circle?" She retorted, "Because it's a pie graph!" Doug, who was also present, asked, "What if it were a triangle?" The words "what if" sparked a lively conversation as different members of the group

Figure 4–9. Malti's graph

Death *is big because 10 people were murdered or die.*
Island *is only a little piece because it as a small problem, they couldn't get to the police.*
Stealing *is big because the murdering tools were stolen from others on the island.*
Judge *is the murderer.*
Crazy people + Death to Death *go in hand. The people on the island were kind of "crazy." Death to Death means the people killed, killed someone else.*
NO ORDER, NO PARTICULAR COLOR

experimented with dividing a triangle. Again, it was not until later that I realized that this discussion had also served as an invitation to explore graphs in a new way. The following week Malti drew a graph for a second Agatha Christie novel. The representation was in the form of a trapezoid divided into numerous triangles. She used her new invention to show that "Everything in the book relates to one thing" [the murder]. A few days later, Malti tried a sketch in the shape of an octagon. Her commentary included two explanations for the shape, "Many sides—many suspects," and "Stop sign because story is almost over." She also repeated another message to her audience, "No special order." As I reviewed these variations of graphs, I realized that one brief, yet playful, conversation inspired Malti to experiment for several weeks.

Malti's many graphs show that she explored the potential of visuals in a personal way while she borrowed from the sketching demonstrations and conversations with her classmates. Our community of learners shared social knowledge or codes, but individuals continued to personalize those codes in unique ways. Ongoing informal talk (Barnes, 1992) and class discussions helped to generate a broad base of shared knowledge in our learning community. Individuals could then draw upon those ideas created in collaboration to invent new personal meanings.

Jill, Doug, and Malti all experimented with adding features to graphs to show details from reading and to solve the problem of averages in graphs. Other students solved the problem of "averages" in different ways. Rachel, for example, had been present during the conversation about "Bad Characters," and she was aware that a limitation of traditional pie graphs was that different degrees of feelings from various points in time could not be shown well. Rachel experimented with a *pair* of pie graphs to signify character changes over time (Figures 4–10a and 4–10b).

In Rachel's' first representation she showed how Jim Hawkins was consumed by four major concerns, which she illustrated in four equal sections. A week later she recorded Figure 4–10b to show her ideas about how Jim's thinking had changed. Although Jim had been concerned about his relationship with Long John Silver earlier in the book, Rachel saw that he was now consumed by worry. She reflected this change in attitude by increasing the proportionate size of Jim's concern about Long John. Creating two representations at different points in time allowed Rachel to compensate for the problem of showing the average of a character's feelings. Studying Rachel's graphs and talking with her about them helped me understand the importance of discussing problems, such as conveying more detail than an average in-depth with learners. Our discussions had served to invite different children to solve the problem in multiple ways, and we all benefited from these many solutions and perspectives.

Figure 4–10a. Rachel's graph

a. These are Jim's thoughts. This shows how he is confused. All of the parts are equal because he feels the same about all of them. I can change parts as time goes on.

Portfolio comment: I chose this peice because I thought it would be good because I could go back in a couple of chapters and look at it. I could change it according to the story.

Reflecting upon the Graphing Experience

I learned a great deal from these students and their classmates as we all explored the potential of graphing. We all knew that graphs show

Figure 4–10b. Rachel's graph sequel

b.

b. These are Jim's thoughts now. This is what I think he is thinking! The sizes of the parts have changed because there have been new things that have happened that could have changed his thoughts. The question marks show he is confused.

overall proportion, that they are intended to be precise, and they are often circular, multicolored, and labeled. The graphs that the students sketched reflected those shared beliefs. Over time, however, the graphs that these and other students created showed unique features of communication that were specific to our classes. These features included combinations of color or careful placement to convey individual events and complex character traits, and multiple graphs to show changes in time. As a class we had created our own unique communication tool, and everyone in the group shared an understanding of the dimensions of the tool that we had created. Through long term collaborative inquiry, we had invented something new.

I also realized that as a teacher, my demonstration as an inquirer was an integral part of our learning community's experience. My interest in particular meaning-making endeavors supported our ongoing conversations. For example, I had been interested in Heidi's placement of size and color of feelings in her *Fallen Angels* graph. My interest in placement led me to question Jill's intentions in her octagonagraph and Malti's interest in this issue followed. In these conversations we had opportunities to borrow from demonstrations of others, and at the same time, to develop patterns of conversation that supported inquiry. We raised questions of intentionality, such as Jill's juxtaposition of sections, and through those questions we opened new avenues to explore. In turn, as the children explained their thinking to me, I was able to return to transcripts of conversations and deepen my understanding of the nature of our learning together.

Part of the understanding that grew from these reflections was my thinking about the patterns of talking together that we developed over time. In our class discussions, questioning intentionality became a shared social norm. Malti acknowledged her awareness of this shared norm in her emphatic statement of, "No color. No particular order." When Jill shared her octagonagraph with a small group, Doug asked her why she had Dr. Livesey as half and half. She answered, "'Cause I felt like it." Doug and Nathan challenged her further by asking, "Why did you think he was bad? Not because you felt like it. You must have had some reason." Nathan knew that in our class we shared an agreement that any of the marks on paper could, perhaps *should*, stand for an idea. In a similar way I (and perhaps others), was expecting Jill to confirm my hypothesis that the placement of the sections in her octagonagraph (Figure 4–6) was significant. Even though Jill answered "no" to my question, Malti seized upon this idea of placement, and she actively pursued this avenue in her sketches.

I also learned that mathematical tools develop in similar ways as tools of art and language. In recent years teachers have tried to foster interdisciplinary connections through theme studies. Most often, the discipline that does not seem to "fit" is mathematics. Using sketching as a means to represent ideas helps mathematical inquiry. Mathematical tools develop out of a need to express meaning, and they are refined collaboratively by a social community through their use over time.

Finally, the story of literature pie graphs demonstrated to me the importance of making sketches public, and talking about those sketches in both formal and informal ways. Sharing and talking served as invitations for future experimentation. When we reviewed pie graphs during our small group meeting, Troy emphasized the social nature of learning by comparing the process of visual artists to that of musicians. "It's like sampling in music. You take something and it gives you an idea of what to do." Doug expressed this value as he described how he built upon Jill's idea of the octagonagraph: "That's what visuals help you do. They can just leave everything open to the reader. If they don't explain it in too much detail, then they can get their own opinion." Certainly we had developed many of our "own opinions" as we explored the many perspectives of literature graphs.

FIVE

Becoming a Risk-taker: One Student's Story

Getting ideas is more important than having ideas.

Doug, *Grade 7*

Few of my students have shown more change in attitude toward risk-taking than Doug. Within the first few days of school I knew that he was a high-achieving student, but I worried about him. I wondered if he felt ownership for his own ideas, or if he simply set his goals to accommodate a teacher's wishes and demands. On many occasions he came to me after dismissal to check directions that I explained in class. He would ask me what "I wanted." I never would have anticipated that by the end of the school year, it would be Doug who would push my thinking about the importance of flexible thinking!

Searching for the "Right" Answer

My first conversation with Doug about a sketch occurred in late September. He was a part of the group that created Figure 1–7 as a group project for *Summer of the Monkeys*, and he approached me after class one day with a draft of his individual project. He had decided to create his own sketch and commentary after working with his group on their poster. He explained that as he collaborated with his group, he had developed this idea, but his group "didn't like

95

it." I thought that he seemed a little nervous as he handed me his sketch. Perhaps he was worried that I, like his group, would not "like" his sketch. His eyes followed my face as I looked at his sketch (Figure 5–1); I guessed that he wanted to see if his work was "right."

After I read the draft, we talked informally about his ideas. I asked Doug if the heart was the biggest figure for a reason. He quoted his text, saying that there was "a lot of love" in the book. I asked if love was the biggest idea in the book. Doug gave examples that did not appear in his written text as he explained the characters' devotion to one another. I told Doug that I was interested in the placement of his symbols. He explained that the hills were on the bottom because "They were the foundation. Everything took place there." The storm needed to be on both sides because, "I didn't want to have it just over Jay Berry or the monkeys because the storm linked both sides." As he prepared to leave for his next class, I suggested that he might reread his draft and reconsider it with our conversation in mind. He seemed flustered by my suggestion. "What do you mean?" he asked, wrinkling his forehead. I sensed that he thought I was judging his paper as inadequate or "wrong." I tried to reassure him by explaining that in our conversation he had added ideas that were not in his essay, such as his elaboration of the idea of "a lot of love" and his idea about the hills. In this conversation I had tried to challenge him to extend his thinking, yet remain sensitive to his fear of risk. I also did not want to take away his ownership of his own text. If he were worried about my reaction to his draft, he might include details that seemed important to me because I was the teacher.

The next day Doug brought a revised draft of his writing to class. The sketch remained the same. The text read:

I put the heart around everything to show that everything in the story took place involving love.

The hills are covering the bottom to show that everything took place on the hills underfoot.

The storm covers the top of the heart because storms are always in the sky. It covers the whole sky because if it were only in part of the sky, then it wouldn't link everything together.

Figure 5–1. Doug's sketch

The main idea of my sketch-to-stretch is how Jay Berry overcame his obstacles of catching the monkeys.

The heart surrounds everything to symbolize that there was a lot of love to help Daisy because he loved her.

The tall brick wall seperates Jay Berry and the monkeys. It keeps him from catching them.

Grandpa is standing on top of the wall helping Jay Berry to overcome his obstacle and catch the monkeys. He is using a steel trap, ideas, and a net to help Jay Berry over.

Jay Berry is thinking of the pony, the .22, and Daisy's leg because he was constantly thinking of those things.

Rowdy is at Jay Berry's side because he is faithful and always in close range of Jay Berry.

Jimbo is in a tree because he was always there. The money signs show that Jimbo and the other monkeys were worth quite a bit of money.

The storm is on both sides of the wall because the storm is what finally linked Jay Berry and Jimbo.

———

The storm is one of the largest turning points in the book. If the storm hadn't happened, other things wouldn't have happened. Daisy and Jay Berry never would have talked that night. The fairy ring never would have grown. The monkeys never would have been caught. Daisy's leg never would have been fixed. Rowdy never would have wished for and gotten his meat rind.

The heart is a bigger theme than the storm because the book was based on love. The storm was only a turning point.

I placed things where I did because that is how the book is set up.

Although Doug included some of the details I had mentioned, such as the placement of the hills and love being the biggest theme, he also elaborated upon his idea of the storm linking both sides and its role as a turning point. He was pleased with his draft. I found out more of his perception of the experience of writing, sketching, and revising when reading his portfolio comment a month later. Doug chose to include this piece as his most significant writing for the first nine weeks. His written reflection read:

I felt that this was my best piece of work because it sounds natural instead of sounding like I tried to make it perfect. It also just came to me. I thought of a good idea and ran with it.

By writing this piece I wanted to share how I felt about the story. I thought I had good, clear views.

Mrs. Whitin helped me very much by showing me how I could make it better and helping me not to worry.

I feel strongest in my illustration. I have always expressed my feelings [better] in pictures than in words. I drew it well enough to show my views of the book.

Taking time to reflect was important for Doug. He realized that through his drafting and conferring he had taken new risks. He "ran with" a lead that seemed exciting. He did not need to have a "right" answer, and he knew it was valuable to reconsider and revise his work. He found that he had clarified his thinking through conversation. He also learned "not to worry": Knowledge can change.

Finding New Ideas Through Sketching

When reading Doug's portfolio commentary about his *Summer of the Monkeys* sketch and essay, I noticed that Doug concentrated on his growth in writing. I wanted to know how he felt about the potential of sketching as well. By November he gave me a glimpse of his thinking in his reflective statement following another collaborative visual. His group had drawn a large hat under which the main character in "Bad Characters" had stuffed shoplifted goods. Doug's reflection revealed that he realized that sketching had enabled him to think about the story in a new way: "When I read the text I didn't realize how much stuff Lottie stole. When we drew the picture, though, I realized how much she stole." Doug's comment showed that he saw benefits of both writing and sketching, and that these perspectives complemented each other.

About a month later Doug showed that he realized that the process of sketching generated new ideas. Early in December I stopped by his desk to read a journal response that he had completed for homework. He had created a sketch (Figure 5–2) to show the conflict in *When the Stars Begin to Fall* (Collier 1986).

As I studied his sketch, Doug remarked that "You get more ideas when you're drawing." I asked him to elaborate. He explained that while writing he thought that he could make a good sketch. As he drew he would think, "That's it," but then he would get more ideas. He pointed to his sketch and said, "At first I was going to draw just a shovel. Then I started thinking about it while I was drawing. I thought of the police car and then I thought of the garbage truck."

I was impressed both with Doug's sketch and with his comments about his authoring process. Through sketching he was able to portray a paradox in the novel. The main character Harry was trying to dig himself out of "garbage"—his family's reputation—while he was being crushed by the "garbage"—or public opinion and gossip. In the story Harry worried about being "trash," which might account for garbage as a symbol. Although Harry was accused of stealing a camera, he was never accused of stealing a shovel. Doug used the shovel as a symbol for the main character's attempt to "dig" himself out of a bad situation,

Figure 5–2. Doug's sketch

This sketch-to-stretch shows that Harry is using a shovel to dig the garbage away from him. The police car shows that the police are on top of him saying that he stole the shovel. Meanwhile, the garbage truck is on top of him dumping garbage on him and making him more trash.

and he combined that symbol with the problem of being accused of stealing. Through drawing and writing he was able to pull significant ideas from the story together. Then, as we talked informally about his sketch, he stepped back and reflected upon the role of drawing in generating ideas. He realized that his idea blossomed in the process of sketching. Knowing the potential of sketching as a tool to discover is an empowering realization. Understanding himself as a maker of ideas was a significant part of Doug's development as a risk-taker. No longer was Doug worried about what "I wanted." He was becoming more and more excited about developing his own ideas and taking credit for the process that led to those discoveries.

Finding the Importance of Collaboration: "I Got My Idea from Jill"

By February Doug was not only taking charge of his own ideas, he was challenging the ideas of his peers. Doug was one of the students who volunteered for the before-school collaborative meeting following the whole class discussion of graphs (Chapter 4). When Jill shared her "octagonagraph" (Figure 4–6), Doug studied the label for the parrot which said "bad." Turning to Jill, he queried in surprise, "The parrot is *bad?*" Jill nodded yes, but Doug was not satisfied. He followed with an assertive, "How do you *know?*" Listening to the transcript of our meeting, I smiled to myself that this boy who had been fearful of my questions in September was now insisting that Jill be specific about her justification for her decision-making! Although I had raised questions about an author's intentions all year, I had never heard Doug take such an active role in pursuing anomalies until this day.

The morning conversation had an immediate impact on Doug. He had never created a pie graph as a response before this occasion, but on the day after our group meeting, he greeted me with, "Look what I did. I got the idea from Jill." He had sketched Figure 4–7, in which he had created strategies to show "more than one thing" by using color, line, placement, and numbers. The large and small group conversations had helped him explore these new ideas. Curious about his thinking, I asked him to tell me more about the process of developing his sketch. He replied he thought it was "a neat idea using the colors and the pie graph to explain about the characters. I didn't want to copy it, so I sat down and thought about it for awhile, and I just went from there. I thought about how you could divide things up into a lot of different categories." Doug had analyzed Jill's graph for its potential, weighed its strengths and weaknesses, and developed it further in his own way. He certainly was not afraid of being "wrong."

Doug decided to put this sketch in his portfolio for the third nine-week period. His written comment added another perspective about his view of that event:

> I chose this response because it showed me how a reader/writer could get ideas from another's writing (Jill's). I also learned that a reader can organize his thoughts by creating a visual.

Doug realized that through collaboration he and his classmates could generate new possibilities for interpretation. Although he saw

Jill's graph as a resource, he invented his own extensions to serve a new purpose. While drawing his graph, Doug realized that he could "organize his thoughts" and pull together ideas in a sketch. Doug's remark helped me to understand more clearly a difference between drawing and writing. Writing is more linear—with a beginning, middle, and an end—but a sketch, graph, or other visual shows a whole. It is easier to see relationships and comparisons in a sketch.

Doug became more playful with visuals after the pie graph discussion. He was present when Malti sketched her pie graph (Figure 4–9) for *And Then There Were None*. I had asked her why she had chosen to represent it in a circular shape, hoping to encourage the group to entertain multiple possibilities of representation. Doug joined in with, "What if it was a triangle? That'd be neat—a triangle graph. What if you had a triangle graph and that looked like this . . . ?" He took a pencil and began to sketch a triangle divided into smaller triangles. He had enjoyed finding new tools for representing his understanding of *Treasure Island*, and he was eager to explore new ideas. His "what if" stance helped him take even more risks.

Role Reversal: Teaching the Teacher

By late March Doug had become confident enough to challenge my thinking as well as his classmates'. The story began when I became interested in another pie graph that Doug had created for the short story "Gaston." I borrowed the sketch overnight to photocopy it, but Doug was worried that it would not copy well, since it was in color. He decided to make me a copy that same evening. While he was making the second sketch, he decided to change it. Figure 5–3 shows the revised graph.

When Doug showed me his revised sketch, we talked informally during recess. I wanted to ask him more about his choice of using temperature and warm and cool colors to signify emotions and if he had developed his ideas as a result of his art class. As we talked, Doug discovered that there was an inconsistency in his categories. At first Doug said that "emotionless" was an absence of feeling, or nothingness. He told me that he had chosen mostly white to show

Figure 5–3. Doug's "Gaston" pie graph

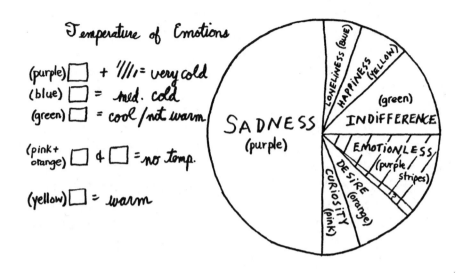

Sadness - Quite a lot of it

Emotionless - Go together, seem to be a lot
Loneliness - Dad seemed lonely

Indifference - There seemed to be a lot of it.
Curiosity - Directed towards Gaston
Desire - Girl desired to see dad, other unknown
Happiness - Mom seemed happy, very little other

———

that, as a feeling, "emotionless" was "in between" cold and warm, but that the purple stripes made "emotionless" seem more cold than warm: "You don't have any feelings. You're not warm or cold feeling, but it still seems kind of cold, don't you think?" Then, as he looked to the key of "temperature of emotions," he saw that he had grouped "emotionless" with "very cold" emotions. This discovery created an anomaly for him. He commented, "You know, I just noticed that some of this I wrote for temperature, and some of it I just wrote for color. I said that white is the absence of color and the absence of feeling, but as I put it for the color it was very cold. If there was an absence of color and everything, then there wouldn't be really temperature either."

At the time, I had difficulty following his thinking, and recess ended. Thinking more about our conversation, I wondered if Doug might be able to resolve this inconsistency through additional conversation. It was this second conversation that proved to be the turning point in our teacher/student relationship. This time Doug's flexible thinking and attitude of inquiry amazed and challenged me in totally unexpected ways. I began the conversation by summarizing his comments about the inconsistency of color and temperature. Then I pushed him to clarify his thinking. "I wondered if you resolved that anomaly. It didn't quite go. I wondered if you had resolved it after you thought about it some more."

Doug studied me quizzically, and answered, "Well, that's not . . . I don't think I'll resolve it, really."

Startled by his calm reply, I persisted, "You didn't resolve it?"

"I don't think I will, either," he continued, "'cause that's the way it is right now, kind of confused. It's always going to be kind of confusing about the color. I mean, there isn't a right or wrong to resolve or anything. It's just always going to be like that."

I was taken aback by his comment. Our roles had completely reversed. I was the one who had tried all year to encourage flexible thinking, and yet here was Doug telling me to tolerate a fascinating anomaly because it encouraged thinking from multiple perspectives! Weakly, I asked, "Is that something to do with visuals? What does that say about visuals?"

Doug answered with assurance, "They don't have to be exact. You don't have to be able to explain every bit of it. They can just leave everything open to the reader if they don't explain it in too much detail. Then they can get their own opinion. That's what came from Jill's. Without having Jill describe every little detail of her visual, it gave me my idea to start my own visual. But if she hadn't left anything up to the reader, it would have been harder to create my own."

Doug showed an amazing tolerance for the absence of clear right and wrong answers here. In fact, he helped me be a more flexible thinker through this conversation. I had expected him to sense the inconsistency of his temperature and color representations and then work it through to "resolve" it. Instead Doug welcomed the ambiguity and saw its value. Doug did not want to be told what to think; he wanted a sketch to be "left open to the reader." Jill's lack of fine detail allowed Doug to invent his own design for expression, and even new purposes for the interpretation of his invention. If he had "resolved" the issue of color and temperature for "emotionless," the graph would have lost its intrigue. I was trying to pin him down, to set limits. In September when I asked him about his *Summer of the Monkeys* draft, I had tried to support him to take multiple perspectives and to extend his thinking. He had tried to pin me down by saying, "What do you mean?" In this conversation the tables had turned. He was challenging *me* not to put limits on his thinking, and he was encouraging me to change my perspective.

"Derek Got His Idea from Me . . . Just Like I Got Mine from Jill"

Toward the end of the year I asked each student to respond to a survey about the sketching strategy: How they went about sketching, when they found sketches useful, and whether they were "easy" or "hard." The students were to imagine that they were writing to the incoming seventh graders. (I routinely have students in the spring leave advice for the new students of the fall.) Doug, deciding that my printed form did not give enough space for his ideas, wrote a page-and-a-half description of his ideas on separate paper. He told me later that he "actually enjoyed writing to the sixth graders." His description revealed his perspective on the process (quoted in part):

To make a sketch, first: always have a PENCIL and piece of paper. Only use a pen when you're sure what you want to do. Next think of anything you're confused about. If you're not confused, just start with a very general topic. Your thinking will branch out until you come upon

105

something you want to write (draw) about . . . Remember: add all details and meaning that you can think of, no matter how small or inobvious. Now, this part is hard to explain. When you sit down to write, you may just write on and on. You won't know where your ideas come from, but write them down.

Doug saw the writing/ drawing process as generative and full of discovery. He said, "Your thinking will branch out" if you start with a "general topic." In this statement he recognized that getting the pencil moving encourages an author to think. Once he has an idea, Doug knows that he needs to concentrate on detail, "no matter how small or inobvious." By trying to include seemingly insignificant thoughts, the author can realize the ultimate beauty of creating: the discovery of unexpected ideas. In this simple description Doug showed this most important principle of authoring. "You won't know where your ideas come from, but write them down."

On the day following the survey, Doug sketched a response to a novel he was reading independently (Figure 5–4). He also included it in his last-quarter portfolio selections. When he showed me the sketch, he commented that he had created it while imagining how a rising seventh grader would read it.

Doug's experience with the survey helped him to look at the strategy of sketching from a new perspective. He enjoyed sharing his expertise with his new audience, the incoming seventh graders. On this same day, he realized a new role in sharing his expertise with his current classmates as well. Doug was in the process of sketching Figure 5–4, while his good friend Derek worked alongside. Derek was sketching a response to *The Westing Game*. As I approached the boys' desks, they covered up their journals, claiming that I "couldn't see yet." Doug announced that he was working on an "awesome" sketch. "Derek has one like it," he continued, "but it's different. He got the idea from me like I got my idea from Jill."

When I looked at both sketches later, I could see their similarity. Derek's (Figure 5–5) also showed aspects of the setting of his book.

As I studied my notes from our conversation and Derek's portfolio reflection I realized that Doug had collaborated with Derek without

Figure 5–4. Doug's *Sharkes in the North Woods or, Nish Na Bosh Na Is Nicer Now* sketch

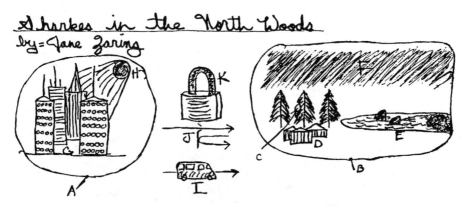

What do you see when you first look at this drawing? I see a truck, a lock, and some skyscrapers. But take a closer look . . .

Now you might see more. Let me explain. (A) and (B) are 'bubbles' around those two sections. They seal off each section. It means that the sections are totally separate. (C) is the North Woods. They are somewhat dark. (D) are the cabins. They have bars (like a prison; that's what they really are.) (E) is the nearby pond. There are SHARK fins on the left (get it?) and pollution on the right. (F) is a dark shadow. Other than the regular shadow in thick woods, there is an evil, sinister shadow (only in the mind). (G) is the city; the homes of the children. (H) is the sun. Their homes are warm & comforting, unlike the shadowy woods. (I) is the bus that links the city to the camp. Next is (J). It shows that the kids are on a one way trip. Going to the camp, they pass freely straight through nonexistant doors. However, going the other way the doors are closed and they are forced to turn back. Last but not least, (K) is a lock symbolizing that the children are prisoners and are locked away in the camp.

Do you see what I mean, now? Good.

Portfolio comment: *I like this response because I wrote it in a way that a new seventh grader could learn something by reading it.*

Figure 5–5. Derek's *The Westing Game* sketch

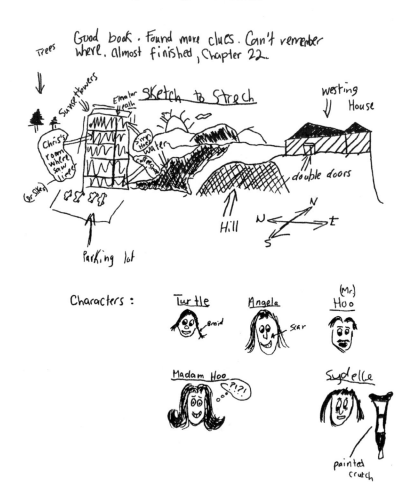

Portfolio comment: *I chose the following Reader's Response because I feel that I learned to draw my visual picture onto paper. It also taught me to research facts about parts of the scene.*

directing him. Instead of telling him what to do, Doug had shared his strategy of recording parts of a scene or setting on paper so that one could gain a new perspective on the relationship among parts. As Doug suggested in his survey, a sketch can help clarify confusing parts of a story. Mystery is the perfect genre for this strategy. Derek drew upon the ideas in Doug's sketch and created his own variation. Doug had followed his own advice that he had shared with me when he described how Jill's octagonagraph had helped him. He had left the idea "open to the reader." He didn't "describe every detail of [his] visual." He encouraged Derek to get an idea to "start his own visual." If he hadn't "left anything up to the reader," whether it was an incoming seventh grader or his current classmate Derek, "it would have been harder to create [their] own." Actions speak louder than words, and Doug's actions that April day reflected his confidence in the process of inventing and sharing ideas in a collaborative community.

Looking Back: Doug's Gifts to Me

Doug helped me strengthen and extend my own theoretical base. Our conversations underscored the importance of informal talk and reflective thought. His work with friends showed me anew the importance of a sense of playfulness with ideas. His growing tolerance for multiple interpretations highlighted the belief that ambiguity serves as an invitation to learners. Doug also helped me think deeply about the relationship between teacher and student. Our mutual quest for creating and expressing ideas redefined our roles. Above all Doug's story showed two overarching ideas. One, by expressing our thinking in multiple ways, such as drawing and writing, we gain a unique perspective on ourselves as learners. Doug was able to see that he generated ideas through drawing and writing alike. He realized that through each medium he enriched his knowing. Secondly, by reflecting on these processes of creating ideas, he became an empowered learner, as demonstrated by his attitude toward himself, his peers, and me. Doug taught me that understanding one's own learning process helps learners to take charge of their learning.

Supporting Risk-taking

Over time Doug learned to articulate his understandings about his own thinking processes and the nature of literacy itself. Continuing to think about his remarkable change in risk-taking, I wondered what conditions encouraged this growth. Thinking about Doug's perceptions of school at the beginning of the year and in the spring, I framed these contrasting perceptions in the following way:

The Two Sides of Risk-taking

Discourage Risk-taking	Encourage Risk-taking
There is one right answer.	There are multiple interpretations of text.
A piece stops with the final draft.	Final drafts can be revisited and revised.
Learning is individual.	Learning is collaborative.
Using the ideas of others is cheating.	Using the ideas of others opens new possibilities.
Outcomes are stated by the teacher.	Learners generate outcomes.
Learning follows a rigid time frame.	Learning follows a flexible time frame.
The teacher poses questions.	Teacher and students pose questions.
Expression of ideas is limited to writing.	Ideas are expressed through multiple communication systems.
The focus of learning is on the product.	The focus of learning is on process.
The teacher evaluates the product.	Teachers and students reflect upon/assess/evaluate process and product.

The first condition that encouraged Doug as a risk-taker was his willingness to participate actively in a wide range of experiences with literature. He read and interpreted his reading through writing and drawing. Secondly, I continually encouraged him to reflect upon his decisions as an author. He regularly shifted between creating and reflecting.

A third condition for promoting this inquiry stance was the learning community of which Doug was a member. None of Doug's experiences occurred in a vacuum. Throughout the school year all learners, including me, challenged one another's thinking by exploring multiple meanings, posing problems, and generating possibilities for inquiry. Through such collaboration, we explored the concept that knowledge is fluid and tentative. We all learned to value the creation of new knowledge.

Although these conditions for inquiry and risk-taking might be identified and discussed individually, it is important to note that all work in concert with one another. Experiences, problem-posing, reflection, and collaboration intertwined over time to create a supportive web for risk-taking. Doug was but one member of the learning community. As he changed, others around him changed, including me. He helped create new knowledge that clearly has challenged me to continue to inquire.

SIX

Sketches as Tools for Reflection

I realize how sketches can be used to clarify something, and to express things more easily and quickly. I have also begun to see how they can be used in everyday life, as when my oboe teacher used a simple visual to illustrate and clarify a point she was making on the benefits of summer lessons.

HEIDI, *Grade 7*

Inviting the students to be co-researchers in my inquiry changed my view of the role of reflection in a learner's life. By contributing their ideas about sketching strategies, the students were becoming increasingly articulate about their own processes of learning. I had always wondered how I as a teacher might best help students be empowered to take charge of their own learning and to understand themselves. I wanted to give students tools for making sense of their world— tools that would go beyond fragmented experiences, that would encourage learners to cycle through ideas, and to make connections between their reading and other experiences.

My experience with Doug challenged my thinking. His story showed me a dramatic example of growth through taking risks, as well as the impact of a student's thinking on my own, but I needed to think hard about what his lessons meant for the larger learning community. Why is reflection important? What happens when individuals and groups step back from learning experiences and look for patterns and principles of learning? I needed to grapple with these questions in order to appreciate the power of teacher research. I knew I was benefiting from my research, but what about the students? Was there a value for them, and if so, what was that value?

Gaining a Perspective on the Nature of Literacy

To understand how the students perceived the process of sketching, I designed a two-part reflective experience to find out more about their thinking. Although I originally thought that this investigation was for my benefit, I found that my plans took unexpected turns and had unanticipated outcomes as they were put into action.

I asked each of the students to complete a survey about their views of the potential of sketching as a tool to respond to literature. A few days later I asked them to sketch representations of the process of creating sketches. Everyone had an opportunity to share drafts with an authors' circle before submitting a final draft sketch. Many of the experiences of those days changed my thinking and strengthened my appreciation for the power of reflection.

Brent, a member of Seth's authors' circle (Chapter 2), created a sketch that caused me to reflect deeply upon key processes of literacy. In his sketch, (Figure 6–1) he expressed in his own way the open potential of reading. The conversation that surrounded his sketch gave me a window to look into the processes through which connected learning occurs.

When Brent brought his sketch to his authors' circle that May day, he had not yet included the whirlwind on the right. He placed his sketch in view of his peers and described:

> First there is a book. When the person thinks of it, the thoughts go into the brain and are transmitted into senses and words. Then you think about the transmission to paper. The cloudy arrow shows the thoughts from the book go into creativity to go back into the book. The stuff at the top is straight from the book. The bottom is

114

Figure 6–1. Visual Cycle

your head, and that makes it creative. Then you're transmitting it
to paper. And the last arrow—you keep reading.

Brent's "Visual Cycle" amazed me. I had been studying the reading process for years, and here a thirteen-year-old could express

deeply theoretical ideas in one concise sketch. To me he was demonstrating Louise Rosenblatt's transactional theory of reading (1978). Brent was showing that meaning does not reside in the text but is created by the transaction between the mind of the reader, or what Brent termed "creativity" and the text. The book is "first," but the book is not absorbed into the mind in a one-to-one correspondence of meaning. The book goes "into the brain" when the ideas are "transmitted into senses and words." In order to further emphasize the active nature of the reader in the construction of meaning, Brent shows through the cloudy arrow "the thoughts go into creativity to go back to the book." Brent's description highlighted the back-and-forth dialogue between the reader and the text. There is a big difference between "the stuff . . . straight from the book" and the point at which the reader "makes it creative." When Brent shared his sketch with his group, I realized that adolescents *do* have the capability to understand and describe the nature of their learning. I began to wonder more about the effects of that capability. What were the benefits of this reflective experience for Brent? I tucked the idea away for further reflection, eager to look for patterns across the experiences of the class.

After Brent spoke, Troy remarked that, "Sometimes you don't understand, so you draw what happens, and you see it on paper." Brent nodded, agreeing that sketching "makes it easier." He explained that the lightning signified how sketches help a reader get ideas.

Seth contributed, "It makes it clearer, and you generate ideas from each other." Troy studied the sketch again and remarked that he liked the arrows. Brent, perhaps combining the ideas of the two remarks, replied that he got the idea of the cycle from a poster of the food chain in science class.

"It's like a graph," mused Troy.

"Yeah, a science graph," concluded Seth.

Jeremy, the fourth member of the group, admitted that at first he didn't realize that part of the sketch was the sky. Brent clarified his intention by explaining that he was trying to show that thinking in this way was "kind of like a dream." Jeremy replied he saw that part of the thinking process as "just ideas swirling around in your head."

Picking up a pencil, Brent said, "That gives me an idea." He then created the whirlwind shape around the storm and lightning.

Now I had more food for thought. I realized that Brent had not created his sketch in isolation. In a similar way that Doug, Jill, and Malti (Chapter 4) developed unique inventions for graphs based upon the experience of the community, Brent had drawn upon ideas from conversations and experiences in and out of class. As Brent used sketches and discussed them over time, he began to look more closely at his world for ideas to communicate his thoughts through drawing. The inspiration for his "Visual Cycle" came from science class. He took the idea of a physical cycle and transformed it into a representation of a mental process. His sketch showed the influence of science class in another way. At the time of this experience, Brent and his classmates were studying the central nervous system, and Brent was obviously intrigued with the mysteries and capabilities of the brain. In a middle school setting where teachers often bemoan the fragmentation of learning and strive to "integrate," Brent's sketch was a sign of ties between classes. Images know no disciplinary boundaries. The class had found that creating pie graphs could signify ideas in literature, and it was not math class. Brent and his classmates were using images from multiple sources as tools to make and share meaning.

I also thought deeply about the role of Brent's authors' circle in his sketch. The boys shared ideas that the class had talked about over the course of several months: that a person sketches in order to clarify ideas ("you don't understand, so you draw what happens, and you see it on paper"), and that by sharing ideas, learners "generate ideas from another person." Seth connected Brent's sketch to the class' experience with graphing by labeling it "a graph." Brent added to Seth's idea when he acknowledged the role of science as well as mathematics in his sketch and remarked, "Yeah, a science graph." Later, when Jeremy admitted that part of Brent's intentions were not clear to him, the ensuing conversation inspired Brent to revise his sketch by adding the whirlwind. Thus the boys not only reflected upon the past experiences of the group, but they simultaneously participated in the process that they were discussing. Brent's sketch became more meaningful as well as physically more detailed through collaboration with his peers. Listening to the earnest tone of their voices, and watching as Brent added the whirlwind to his paper, I wondered if some of the power of this experience was a feeling of empowerment on the part of the boys. They were excited by their discoveries about themselves and the way they learned.

A few weeks later, these boys and their classmates reflected upon their growth during the course of the year as they composed "learning autobiographies" as part of their last portfolio entries. I stated as a requirement that they discuss their learning through reading, writing, speaking, and listening, but I did not specifically ask them to include their views about sketching. Each boy, however, felt that sketching and discussing sketches had played an important part in their growth over the year, as evidenced by these excerpts from their writing:

Brent
I think Mrs. Whitin helped me change in different ways. At first, I didn't even know we could have such an open class discussion. Discussions that had ideas change, and thoughts that would be taken to a more specific thought. My use of visuals were a dramatic change . . . I learned different ways to use them. I also picked up ideas from other students. I also was amazed at what can come out of a visual.

Jeremy
Another way I've grown is to organize my thinking on paper with the ways you taught me. All of these ways are good, but I like sketch-to-stretch the best because I like drawing and having different ideas.

Seth
Reader's responses helped me get more involved with the character. It showed me through design and color what that character was really like. I think throughout my eighth grade year I will do reader's responses to help clear up the plot, the idea, or even characters.

These boys saw that their response to literature had changed, such as getting "more involved with the character." They had learned a strategy that they saw as valuable to them—to organize ideas or to

118

"clear up" the elements of plot, ideas, or characters. Finally, they realized the power of a community of learners—they "picked up ideas from other students" or through discussion the entire group could realize a "more specific thought." Reflecting upon their comments, I came to see the importance not only of sharing powerful literature but also of taking time to step back from our experiences with that literature to understand what made it significant to us. These boys left in May with refined tools for learning, and, although this realization of the value of reflection to students was important, it was only half the story. As a part of the community, I, too, was changed as a learner, and the students played an active role in my own new dimensions of learning.

Teacher as Learner: My Own "Sketch of Sketching"

As Donald Graves (1983) and others have so often stressed in Writers' Workshop, it is important for teachers to write along with their students. In a similar vein, since I saw sketching as parallel to authoring written texts, I knew that I needed to participate in the process of creating sketches. I did so from time to time during the course of the year, but I realized a new dimension of this participation when I drew my own "sketch of sketching."

I worked on two drafts at home the night before the children sketched their ideas and shared them with authors' circles. I didn't want to be influenced by the children's sketches initially, although I did plan to confer with students in an authors' circle of my own. Creating my drafts challenged me. I wanted to convey my understandings of both the theory I had read and of my classroom observations and interviews, and I had to think very hard of ways to signify my ideas without language. As I sketched, I appreciated even more fully the complex thinking this strategy requires. I made two sketches because neither one showed all of the concepts and relationships I wanted to represent. I was eager to hear what my students—my co-researchers—would think, but I put my sketches aside for a few days and turned my attention to the students' drafts and revisions.

After the students had had a chance to develop their sketches and talk about them in class, I invited my "before-school collaborators" to examine mine. I showed them my drafts—a spider web and a tree—and briefly explained the thinking behind each. The students encouraged me to pursue the tree draft, which surprised me initially— I had preferred my spider web. Jill insisted, "A spider web, to me . . . if you handed that to me and told me to figure it out, it would take forever and ever and ever and ever. And this one—the tree—is easy to figure out. You can tell the roots are in the book and giving you all these feelings and ideas." Thus, even initially Jill and her classmates served that all-important role of an authors' circle: to allow the author to gain a better sense of how one's intentions are interpreted by an audience. They helped me make myself clear. My tree draft, partially revised by students during my authors' circle, is found in Figure 6–2.

I explained the meaning of the tree to the group in this way:

I have a tree, and I was thinking that the roots of the tree is the book, but then the roots are also what you like to do, or what you love, or what your interests are—what your ideas are and your thinking, and your relationships with other people and your culture. That's the United States, but it's kind of hard to see. Troy, I'll need to commission you to draw. And it all comes up inside, you know, what you're doing, and what comes in sort of comes out, like it comes out in the way you relate to people. In your visual you do it by collaboration and symbols that you're familiar with, like people have used greater than or less than, or exclamation points, and some people have used shapes. Then you get further ideas, and this is an acorn, and it all goes into the ground and something new happens. What I wanted to show was a cycle.

After we decided to focus on the tree draft, the students began to offer ideas to elaborate upon my sketch. Doug suggested that I should add some leaves because leaves "would be the little ideas that branch off the big ones, but aren't big enough to be an acorn." Jill agreed, remarking that as it stood, the tree looked like a dead tree.

120

Figure 6–2. Tree

"Yeah," Doug chimed in, building upon his leaf metaphor, "and ideas aren't dead." Already my thinking was being stretched, and I was seeing the potential of the tree sketch in a new light. I had not considered how the tree might show the relationship among ideas, or that my sketch might make ideas look lifeless. We next turned to the acorn and debated whether an acorn or an apple tree might be more appropriate. Although apples might be more colorful and

121

attractive, we decided upon the acorn. Doug quoted the familiar saying of "the mighty oak," adding that "A little idea can be big." I glanced at the roots of the tree, where I had tried to convey the idea that we draw upon our shared cultural experience in order to share our meaning with others. Surely the same phenomenon was happening during the authors' circle, as it had with Brent's and others. All of us at the meeting shared an understanding of the cycle of a tree, and we all were familiar with the saying of the "mighty oak." By putting these familiar ideas into a new context, however, we opened a new potential of understanding. The concrete image of a tree was encouraging us to talk about complex, abstract ideas.

One of the reasons I had preferred the web initially was because in that sketch I could more easily show that all of our ideas were connected to one another. I thought that this feature was extremely significant, so I wanted to include it in my tree sketch in some way. Doug insisted that ideas don't always have to come back together, that they "can be their own ideas." He was stressing the importance of variety in experience and thinking. Next Troy pointed out that with a tree all the branches do connect in a sense. A tree "spreads out, like those big trees in the old neighborhoods. You can see it looks just like a big circle with a trunk. In a way, they all do connect."

His perspective caused me to reflect, and I mused, "Because as you step back—so if you step back from a tree and look at it, it all goes like a whole, but if you get close you can see what the parts are." As I listened to Troy, and as I worked to put my ideas into words, I saw the tree in a different symbolic light. I believed that all aspects of language, for example, work together in concert, yet it is important to highlight one of those features, in order to understand it more in depth. In a similar way the tree showed us the unified whole of our experience, and as we stepped closer to examine the parts, we never fully lost the importance of their being connected to the whole as a tree. Even though I had worked hard to convey my philosophy in my draft, Troy's simple comment encouraged me to reflect anew upon my entire belief system of how people learn and how we should teach.

However, I also valued Doug's idea which to me signified the importance of an individual's unique inventions and creations. As I struggled to put my thoughts together, I continued, "All right, let's think . . . the whole is one thing, and it's okay, like you say, Doug, to have lots of little ideas, but sometimes you pick up ideas from each other, like you, Jill, with the octagonagraph, and Doug's and Malti's spun off of that. Different people went in different directions from it, so even though that was a distinct idea, it influenced others." The conversation was forcing me to reorganize my thinking, to connect in a meaningful way my belief system, Doug's insights, and their relationship to the metaphor of the tree that I had sketched. Reflecting upon this conversation later, I realized that the metaphor of the tree served as an anchor to our thoughts. Everyone in the group shared an understanding of trees, how they look, and how they grow. This familiar image allowed us to talk in complex ways about abstract ideas. The tree also helped focus our thinking while we offered our various perspectives. As each person contributed an idea, we related that idea to our metaphor.

As Jill thought about the notion of connecting ideas, she saw the trunk symbolically; it was the trunk that connected all of the ideas. Her comment shifted our thinking; we realized that we could develop new insights if we considered a downward movement toward the roots, rather than the upward movement of the growing branches. Doug commented that ideas "could go back down to the book," pointing to the book tucked among the roots. Jill expanded upon Doug's idea by saying that it is the brain that connects a person's ideas with the features of an experience represented by the symbols in the roots. Her comment triggered a new connection in my mind to Brent's visual cycle. I wondered how my sketch could convey the notion of a reader being an active constructor of ideas and being changed through experiences, as Brent had done with his cloudy and clear arrows. The children were helping me be more reflective about my own work. We were equals in this literary endeavor. We all needed each other and the image of the tree to generate new ideas and to consider alternative perspectives.

I asked Troy, who had been part of Brent's authors' circle, to help me explain Brent's thinking to the group. The others agreed on the importance of the active role of the reader to my sketch. Jill noted that "part of the book is in each tree, and a part of your brain is in each tree." Stacey continued, "If you were drawing the tree (from the acorn), you could draw it smaller or bigger or different. It would show change, 'cause every time you do something like a reader's response, you kind of feel different about the book 'cause you understand it more."

Doug, who had been waiting for a turn to speak, added a new idea to show thoughts returning to a book. The idea of "going down" caused him to think of lightning striking a tree. He commented, "What happens when a tree gets hit by a lightning bolt? It hits the branches and goes back all the way to the roots. If it doesn't kill the tree, it could show how it goes back to the roots." Doug's qualifying statement about "if it doesn't kill the tree" showed his continued concern with "ideas aren't dead," as well as his interest in the movement from a reader's ideas "back to the book." I wondered aloud if we should add lightning, and Doug offered an additional meaning for lightning, that it could signify brainstorming. Once again we were generating new ideas through our exploratory talk. Troy picked up a pencil and began to sketch lightning. The group considered the placement of the lightning and what its placement might signify. We collectively decided that the lightning should be near the acorn so that it would show that brainstorming leads to new ideas. Our discussion of lightning had connected the two ideas of a person changing thoughts through collaboration and the generation of new ideas. I realized that as a group we were making something new collaboratively. I began to see that taking time to reflect on one's learning is important for each individual, for the teacher, and for the entire learning community. The earnest tone in the students' voices clarified for me the value of negotiating meaning with the teacher. I could sense a feeling of empowerment among the group. They knew that they were challenging my thinking; all of our understandings were enriched by our conversation.

As Troy continued to sketch, Doug studied the branches that I had drawn. Trying to expand upon the importance of creating new ideas, he commented to the group, "You know how all the branches are sort of open-ended? I was thinking about a tree, and you know how branches all come to a close? Well, your tree ought to be weird. They shouldn't close, 'cause none of the ideas really are dead-ended." As Doug spoke, I realized that once again the group was extending the meaning of a sketch beyond its original intent. I had not intended to convey any special meaning by having my branches open-ended, yet through our discussion of ideas, we had collectively created a symbol with a new meaning. My sketch had served as a vehicle to develop ideas, and at the same time the ideas developed my sketch.

Doug's last comment had shifted our attention; we focused once more on the branches. As I looked at them, I realized that our conversation had raised some new concerns for me as an author. I had placed symbols within the outline of various branches, which represented the role of art, mathematics, and community in the expression of ideas and in the generation of new perspectives and ideas. I wondered if the placement of the symbols would enable us to describe the relative importance of these features. I asked the students to describe which branch (i.e. which feature of authoring) they felt was most powerful. Their comments helped me to reflect upon both my sketch and the process of collaboration that we had just experienced. Jill insisted that, "Number one is the influences people give you. Because like no matter what you think, you're always going to change your mind when somebody tells you something about the book. You're going to go, 'Oh!' and then you're going to scratch out whatever you have, and you're going to redo it." The other members of the group agreed. Doug contributed that the acorn should be next in importance, "'Cause getting new ideas is more important than having ideas."

To me, these two students' comments symbolized that morning's authors' circle. I had created a sketch, and I had worked hard to convey my beliefs in a clear, insightful manner. While talking with these young people, however, my own mind cried, "Oh!" and I had reorganized my ideas. I had mentally "scratched out" what I had, and together we revised both my written sketch and my thinking. I had had some significant ideas, but it was the process of "getting new ideas" that was "more important." That morning my authors' circle and I had planted a new acorn.

I have thought a great deal about that day, and each time that I review the transcript of the conversation, I revise and expand my thinking. I have come to have a new appreciation for collaboration and for metaphor. The metaphor of the tree caused us all to frame familiar ideas in a new context, and we generated new insights from this reframing. We used the metaphor as a tool to talk about complex ideas. Many of these ideas might seem above a thirteen-year-old's capability; it was the concrete image that supported the creation of these abstract ideas. However, I did not use my sketch as a vehicle to lecture them about my ideas; instead, we made meaning together, and the views of the students changed my thinking. I was an active learner in the group. Despite our differences in age and experience, we contributed equally to the creation of new insights and connections. Together we explored the meaning of an extended metaphor and developed several important ideas about literacy. The whole of our community was greater than the sum of its parts.

Over time I saw a second benefit of this kind of theoretical discussion as well. When I began to study the process of sketching ideas from literature, I had been concerned about not being fair to the students' use of time. Having the students sketch their perceptions of the process and having them reflect upon my tree sketch allowed me to see the value of sharing one's research with students. Through sketching and talking, I saw that the students had gained a new perspective of their own learning. Through sketches such as Seth's (Chapter 2), they saw connections between authoring writing and authoring art. They came to value the importance of collaboration and the influence of another's ideas upon one's thinking. Their view of "right" and "wrong" had changed; they weren't embarrassed to say, "Oh!" and "scratch it out." Finally, as Doug said, they didn't view knowledge as static or "dead-ended." These comments indicated to me that these students had taken charge of their own learning in a new way. They were empowered learners who understood their own processes of literacy and the strategies that best encouraged these processes. I no longer was afraid that teacher research was an egotistical venture that benefited me alone. By inviting the students to inquire with me, I was supporting their growth and independence as well.

Using Sketches to Reflect upon Personal Growth

The experience with the "sketches of sketching" opened new doors for me. I began to wonder how to use sketches as a tool for reflection in other ways. The students were creating portfolios in which they collected and evaluated selected pieces of their work during the course of the year. At the year's end I customarily asked students to write a "learning autobiography" in which they described their growth as a literate person. Heidi's comment at the beginning of this chapter is an excerpt from her final reflective essay. She connected the use of sketches as a strategy to part of her learning life outside of the classroom, and her comment further inspired me to develop a new plan. The year after our experiences with reflective sketches, I invited students to include a sketch with their learning autobiography. Several students were intrigued with the idea. When I read their pieces and examined their sketches, my belief in the power of creating metaphors for learning was confirmed in new ways. I was interested to find that two of the students had chosen to sketch a tree to represent their growth.

Ron's sketch emphasized a theme of blossoming (Figure 6–3). Ron saw his growth as a blossoming tree. He realized that his past was a foundation, that the roots and trunk symbolized a potential, but the "fruits" appeared during the course of the year. Within each leaf he sketched symbols such as a person gazing into a mirror and seeing not only the reflection, but through the mirror to "the truth" behind it. This representation showed me that Ron saw himself as an active, probing constructor of meaning. Like Brent and his "Visual Cycle," Ron recognized his contribution to meaning; the text did not "reflect back" the truth without Ron's interpretation of it. Through his sketch

Figure 6–3. Ron's tree

This year I have grown like a tree, from a scraggily mess of roots, a trunk, and bare branches to a tree full of lush leaves.

One of my new leaves is the fact that I can find symbolism in books that I would have normally taken for face value. Now, I can look behind the reflection in the mirror and see the truth. It would have never occured to me at the beginning of the year, that Eve Bunting's "The Terrible Things" had anything to do with the Holocaust.

My ability to write with different perspectives is another leaf. Earlier in the year I might have written—A dog attacked me unexpectedly as I was walking down the street.—Now, I might write—Grrrr, Ahhhh, I could feel my flesh being torn and scratched. I was screaming and being thrashed around, and I didn't even know what was happening. When I finally pulled myself up, I saw blood trickling out everywhere. I looked up just in time to see a dog turning the corner—

Ever since I was in about third grade I never had any problem speaking and giving reports. This school year I would practically or actually turn red, just presenting a reader's response. I am just recently getting out of this habit.
I, the tree, have also had fruits, personal satisfaction and awards such as work being published in Images *(the school literary magazine).*

Ron also celebrated his growth as a writer, and he acknowledged his journey through adolescent self-consciousness toward a new self-confidence.

Erin used a series of trees to show her growth over time (Figure 6–4). Erin had used the tree to symbolize both her growth during the year and her potential growth in the future. Her sketch emphasized the upward, reaching growth of the sapling as well as its branching out in new directions, while Ron's had focused on the "fruits" of the year. For both of these students, expressing their evaluation of their growth in multiple ways enhanced their understanding of themselves. Like the students who authored the "sketches of sketching," Erin and Ron understood the processes of their own literacy. They had developed tools that connected experiences together and that enabled them to take charge of their own learning.

The cycle for me as a teacher continued as well. When I read these two essays and studied the sketches, I thought back to my experience the previous year with my tree sketch. I now could incorporate some of Ron's and Erin's images, such as the growth from a seedling to a sapling, or the bearing of fruits, into my understanding of my sketch. The tree was a reference point for my thinking; I could revisit earlier ideas as I wove new connections to my image. I, too, was continuing to grow and to see new potential for using sketches as a tool for reflection.

Reflecting on Reflection

As I have found so often, the children led the way to my growth in understanding. When I first began to pursue my interest in visual

129

Figure 6—4. Four trees

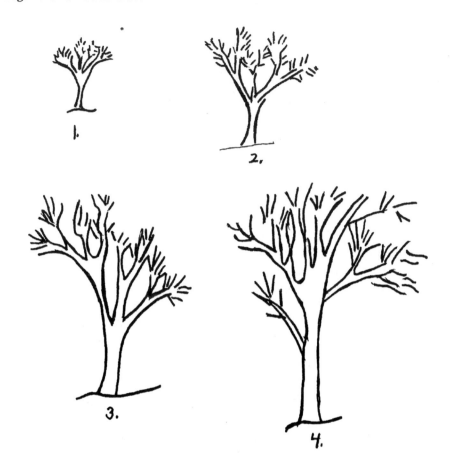

(1) This small seedling represents me at the beginning of the year. I was small in my scope of Language Arts. I only wrote humor for freewrites. I was a little uncomfortable with reader's responses. My first response doesn't show much depth of thinking. It was on Summer of My German Soldier. In it, I only talked about my feelings in response to the events in the book. I didn't say anything about why these events might have happened, or how the characters felt about them. I was surprised with the idea that books could have specific themes, like relationships or racism. I was scared of symbolism. I thought something could symbolize only one thing, and if my answer was different, I was wrong. I didn't like stories that I didn't understand. At that time, I would rather say I hated a story than read it again and try to understand it. But I had the potential to grow . . .

(2) After the first nine weeks had passed, I had definitely shown some growth. I started using visuals to respond to literature. This was a new skill for me. I started using symbolism in my visuals. I wasn't afraid of it anymore because I knew it was interpretive. For example, a poem that uses symbolism can mean something different for everyone. My reader's responses were much deeper. I talked about character relationships, universal issues, and personal choices. I discussed these responses with groups. I realized that saying I hated a story because really I didn't understand it was a way of saying "I quit." So I tried to gain a deeper understanding of stories before I passed judgement on them, especially in Junior Great Books. I gained knowledge in spelling, grammar, and mechanics. I also learned how to loop. But I had had room for new growth . . .

(3) By the beginning of 1993, I was finally starting to write about serious topics without humor. Two examples of this were my pieces about the State Meet and a possible move from Columbia. I had even tried a little poetry. A new strategy of starting with a kernel of truth helped me branch off into fiction. Some of my work had been published in the literary magazine, which made me very proud. In January, I met Long John Silver, on whom some of my deepest thinking was spent, and who inspired my first 3-D visual. Now I was looking for symbolism in books I read, making each book special to me. But I wasn't finished growing yet . . .

(4) I've come a long way since August last year. I've overcome my fear of symbolism, learned to make visuals, how to use Writing Assistant on the computer, and become a deeper writer. I've written about deeply hurting things. I've started to make decisions about where I stand on important issues that will affect me as an adult. I still haven't mastered poetry, but I haven't given up. I want to write more, possibly longer stories. I haven't stopped growing. I've got a long way to go. I'm only a small sapling.

—————

response to literature, I had worried about putting my research before the students' learning. As I considered the role of students as co-researchers, however, I realized that I had developed a deeper understanding of the process of reflection as well as its power.

First, I saw the role of reflection as twofold. Reflection encourages learners to make connections among experiences, thereby understanding relationships and underlying principles of those experiences.

Seth and his authors' circle, for example, saw the relationship between authoring art and authoring a written text as they stepped back from their experience to reflect upon it. Reflection also enables learners to understand themselves as meaning-makers. Seth remarked in his learning autobiography that "getting involved with the characters" was important to him as a reader.

The process of reflection led both the students and me to talk theoretically about learning. The benefit to me as a professional educator was obvious, but I came to realize that understanding the process of learning is empowering to students as well. When Heidi realized that visuals could be a tool for organizing or clarifying thoughts outside of language arts class, she changed as a learner. At the end of her seventh grade year she had more control of her learning because she understood how tools of communication might best work for her.

Taking a theoretical stance with one's teacher is empowering to students as well. As we analyzed my sketch of the tree, the students realized that their views were changing both my sketch and my understanding of its meaning. They saw themselves as creators of ideas. I had stumbled upon this understanding of the value of sharing unintentionally, but it has changed my view of teaching forever. I now listen to students with an even more sensitive ear than I had ever dreamed could be possible.

Finally, my appreciation for the role of metaphor in creating and sharing ideas grew tremendously through these experiences. Sketching is metaphorical, and creating sketches forces authors to consider ideas from a new perspective. Brent chose to use the physical cycle of the food chain to create the abstract "visual cycle" of making meaning from a printed text. When I developed my two drafts for my sketch of sketching, I struggled with the challenge of framing my learning theory into nonlinguistic symbols. I considered the potential of every mark on the paper: size, placement, number, proportion, line, and so forth in relation to what I believed about learning. Later when I shared my sketches with my students, the views of others sent my mind "back to the drawing board" for reconsideration and revision. The sketch of the tree and the model of a cycle served as anchors to the sensory world as we discussed abstract ideas. By using sketching as a tool for reflection, I have come to conclude that metaphor is the root of abstract thinking. My new understanding is setting me on new paths of inquiry. As Erin stated simply yet eloquently, "I'm only a small sapling."

References

Professional

BARNES, D. [1976] 1992. *From Communication to Curriculum*. Portsmouth, NH: Boynton/Cook Publishers.

EISNER, E. 1985. *The Art of Educational Evaluation: A Personal View*. Philadelphia: The Falmer Press.

———. 1992. "The Misunderstood Role of the Arts in Human Development." *Phi Delta Kappan* 73 (April): 591–595.

GRAVES, D. 1983. *Writing: Teachers and Children at Work*. Portsmouth, NH: Heinemann.

HARSTE, J. & SHORT, K., WITH BURKE, C. 1988. *Creating Classrooms for Authors*. Portsmouth, NH: Heinemann.

MURRAY, D. 1968. *A Writer Teaches Writing: A Practical Method of Teaching Composition*. New York: Houghton Mifflin.

ROSENBLATT, L. 1978. *The Reader, the Text, the Poem: The Transactional Theory of a Literary Work*. Carbondale, IL: Southern Illinois Press.

SHORT, K. & BURKE, C. 1991. *Creating Curriculum: Teachers and Students as a Community of Learners*. Portsmouth, NH: Heinemann.

VYGOTSKY, L. 1978. *Mind in Society*. Cambridge, MA: Harvard University Press.

WHITIN, P. 1994. "Opening Potential: Visual Response to Literature." *Language Arts* 71 (8): 101–107.

Literature

BRADBURY, R. 1987. "All Summer in a Day." In *McDougal Littel Literature*, revised edition. Evanston, IL: Schoffrath & Sternberg.

BRIDGERS, S. 1979. *All Together Now*. New York: Alfred A. Knopf, Inc.

BUNTING, E. 1989. *The Terrible Things*. Philadelphia: The Jewish Publication Society.

CHRISTIE, A. 1977. *And Then There Were None*. New York: Berkeley.

CLEAVER, W. & CLEAVER, V. 1969. *Where the Lilies Bloom*. New York: J.P. Lippincott.

COLLIER, J. 1986. *When the Stars Begin to Fall*. New York: Doubleday.

GREENE, B. 1973. *Summer of My German Soldier*. New York: Bantam Books.

INNOCENTI, R. 1990. *Rose Blanche*. New York: Stewart Tabor & Chang.

MYERS, W. 1988. *Fallen Angels*. New York: Scholastic.

PATERSON, K. 1991. *Lyddie*. New York: Viking Penguin.

RASKIN, E. 1978. *The Westing Game*. New York: Dutton.

RAWLS, W. 1961. *Where the Red Fern Grows*. New York: Doubleday.

———. 1976. *Summer of the Monkeys*. New York: Doubleday.

SAROYAN, W. 1984. "Gaston." In *Junior Great Books, Series Seven 2*. Chicago, IL: The Junior Great Books Foundation.

STAFFORD, J. 1984. "Bad Characters." In *Junior Great Books, Series Seven 1*. Chicago, IL: The Junior Great Books Foundation.

STEVENSON, R. [1895] 1981. *Treasure Island*. New York: Dell.

TAYLOR, M. 1977. *Roll of Thunder, Hear My Cry*. New York: Dial.

———. 1990. *The Road to Memphis*. New York: Dial.

References

Voigt, C. 1981. *Homecoming.* New York: Atheneum.

——— . 1983. *Dicey's Song.* New York: Atheneum.

Zaring, J. 1982. *Sharkes in the North Woods or, Nish Na Bosh Na Is Now.* Boston: Houghton-Mifflin.